THE ART

OF THE

OLD ENGLISH POTTER.

THE ART

OF THE

OLD ENGLISH POTTER

BY

L. M. SOLON

ILLUSTRATED WITH FIFTY ETCHINGS BY THE AUTHOR

With a new Introduction by
Michael R. Parkinson

EP Publishing Limited
1973

First published 1883 in a limited
edition of 260 copies

ISBN 0 85409 840 2

Please address all enquiries to EP Publishing Ltd.
(address as above)

Printed in Great Britain by
The Scolar Press Limited, Menston, Yorkshire

INTRODUCTION

Marc Louis Solon, the author of this book, *The Art of the Old English Potter*, was born at Montauban in France in 1835 and came to England to settle in 1871. Before coming to this country he had studied at the Elementary School of Design in Paris and developed an interest in decorative and applied art. He was invited to work at the famous porcelain factory at Sèvres. On the outbreak of the Franco-Prussian War, M. Solon emigrated to England hoping to join the distinguished English firm of Mintons, who made some of the finest of English porcelains. M. Solon was successful in this purpose and eventually succeeded J. L. F. Arnoux, another Frenchman, as the Art Director at Mintons, where he developed a decorative technique called pâte-sur-pâte, which he had learned at Sèvres and which will be referred to again. This book, however, is devoted to a kind of ceramics completely different from that which M. Solon himself made, namely English pottery from early times to the middle of the eighteenth century.

In the preface, Marc Solon describes in an extremely fascinating way how he first came by chance to be interested in and collect English pottery. Probably many collectors began in a similar manner, having stumbled unexpectedly upon some piece which appealed to their interest but about which they knew nothing. The two 'strange-looking' pieces of salt-glaze which M. Solon saw through the cottage window in the North Staffordshire countryside when he was taking his customary 'perambulations' on the Saturday half holiday, were to be the first in a remarkable and important collection of English pottery. Several records of this collection were made: M. Solon wrote articles in early numbers of *The Connoisseur*; the collection was catalogued finally for the sale at Charles Butters in Hanley in 1912; an undated list by Solon himself describing his 'collection of old English pottery with a few examples of similar styles of manufacture but of foreign origin' and the fifty pieces described and illustrated in the second half of his book.

M. Solon writes on p. ix of his Preface: 'The purpose I had in view when I began to sketch some of my pieces, was to make them known to a few far-away friends, for we all like to draw others into sharing our own tastes, and it is with all of us a pet weakness to discourse and convert. This explains how, by slow degrees, I was led to etch the most interesting specimens of my collection, and subsequently came to think of publication'. The illustrations, therefore, are also Solon's own work. With each etching is a page of text describing the pots depicted. The attractive binding of the first edition of the book*, which was limited to two hundred and sixty copies, was also designed by the author himself, and incorporates a 'Staffordshire slipware dish and cradle' and a 'Wrotham candlestick'. In the Preface the author also explains the purpose of the book as an account of English pottery, stating '. . . that my ambition never went so far as to attempt a complete history of English Pottery.' and 'The principal object of this essay will be to relate, . . . the efforts and trials of the first plodders in the field, the unknown ones, who have no special history of their own, but who, working as a group, made the ground ready for the splendid achievements of the great potters of the latter part of the eighteenth century.' M. Solon also explains that he does not intend to go beyond the middle of the eighteenth century, writing that 'I shall close my account at the coming of the prince of English potters . . .'. He gives a brief summary of the headings under which the history will be written, beginning with Early Pottery and ending with early Cream Colour, '. . . the first step towards the white earthenware which, brought by Josiah Wedgwood to the highest degree of perfection, was to supersede all others.' Marc Solon gives the reader a very good reason for choosing to illustrate pots from his own collection; the pieces had not previously been published and he was avoiding representing pots to be seen in public museums. The Solon Collection was one of the greatest collections of English Pottery and the fifty pots chosen and etched by the author are a very interesting selection, illustrating not only each part of the history but also each part of his collection.

The Art of the Old English Potter was first published in 1883 and is one of the great early books published on this subject. The book was

*See reproduction following this introduction.

dedicated to Colin Minton Campbell, and printed by Bemrose and Sons of Derby, Mr. Bemrose being a collector and writer himself. This book and the large and remarkable collection Marc Solon formed are a great tribute to the English potters by a Frenchman who was a great potter in a very different style. There is, at the end of his discussion of slipware, a very interesting comparison made by M. Solon. 'May we be excused,' he writes, 'if we show ourselves a little partial to the Slip process, considering that it is closely connected with "Pâte-sur-Pâte", a process that we have practised ourselves for more than twenty-five years, and which is also painting in Slip upon the unbaked surface?'. (p. 41).

On page viii of the Preface M. Solon laments, as others have done, the dispersal of the collection formed by another, earlier, famous potter, Enoch Wood of Burslem, a collection which he tells us '. . . became the model of what . . . I had tried to emulate.' Marc Solon's own collection was dispersed at a sale held in the salerooms of Charles Butters in Hanley from 26th to 28th November 1912, and this, too, is a matter of regret, but the fine sale catalogue is a very good record of this early and important collection.

Marc Solon was not only a collector of pottery, but also of books on the subject of ceramics, and his very large and valuable library, containing rare and important works, was fortunately preserved intact, first for many years as part of the Library of the North Staffordshire Technical College and more recently in the Reference Library of the City Libraries, Stoke-on-Trent.

In addition to *The Art of the Old English Potter*, Marc Solon wrote many other books on pottery and porcelain, which have remained classics: *A Brief History of Old English Porcelain and its Manufactories*, *A History and Description of Italian Maiolica*, *A History and Description of Old French Faience* and *The Ancient Art Stoneware of the Low Countries and Germany*; he also compiled a very useful index: *Ceramic Literature, An Analytical Index*.

Potter, collector of pots and books on pottery and porcelain, student of and writer on the ceramic art; had Marc Louis Solon been only one of these, he would have had a distinguished and honoured place, but he was all of them, which is indeed very remarkable, and all students will always be in his debt.

Walking was once a more customary activity than it is now, bringing indirect as well as direct benefits; Marc Solon's predilection for Saturday afternoon 'perambulations' in particular brought him and us unexpected and considerable rewards.

Monsieur Solon died at his home in Stoke on 23 June 1913 and some months later Robert L. Hobson of The British Museum gave the Memorial Lecture to the English Ceramic Society. Mr. Hobson said then of the work of M. L. Solon, 'Though his own creations were so cultured and classical, he yielded to none in his admiration of the quaint old English pottery, which he not only collected assiduously, but celebrated in a delightful book illustrated by his own superb etching.'

MICHAEL ROBERT PARKINSON

Endon, Staffordshire, and Manchester.
JUNE, 1973

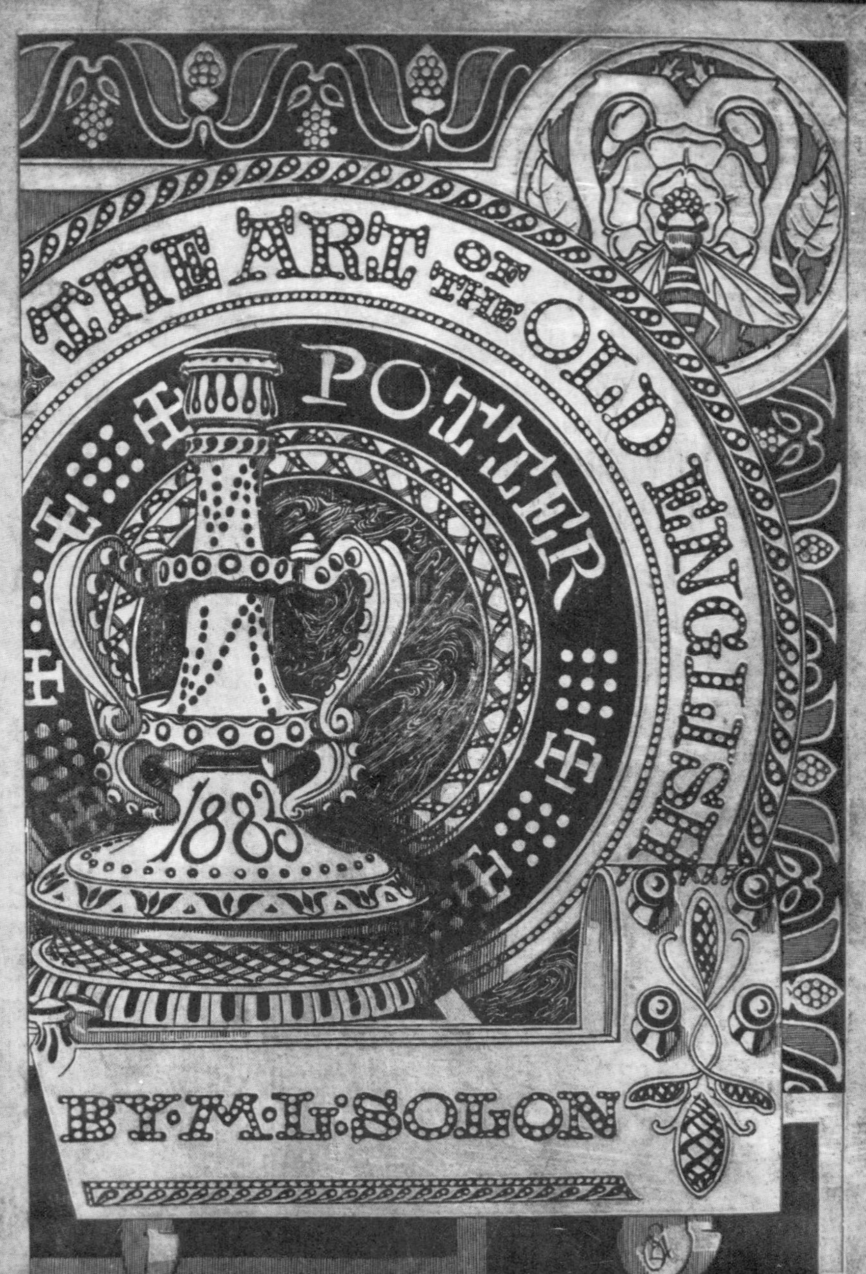
THE ART OF THE OLD ENGLISH
POTTER
1883
BY·M·L·SOLON

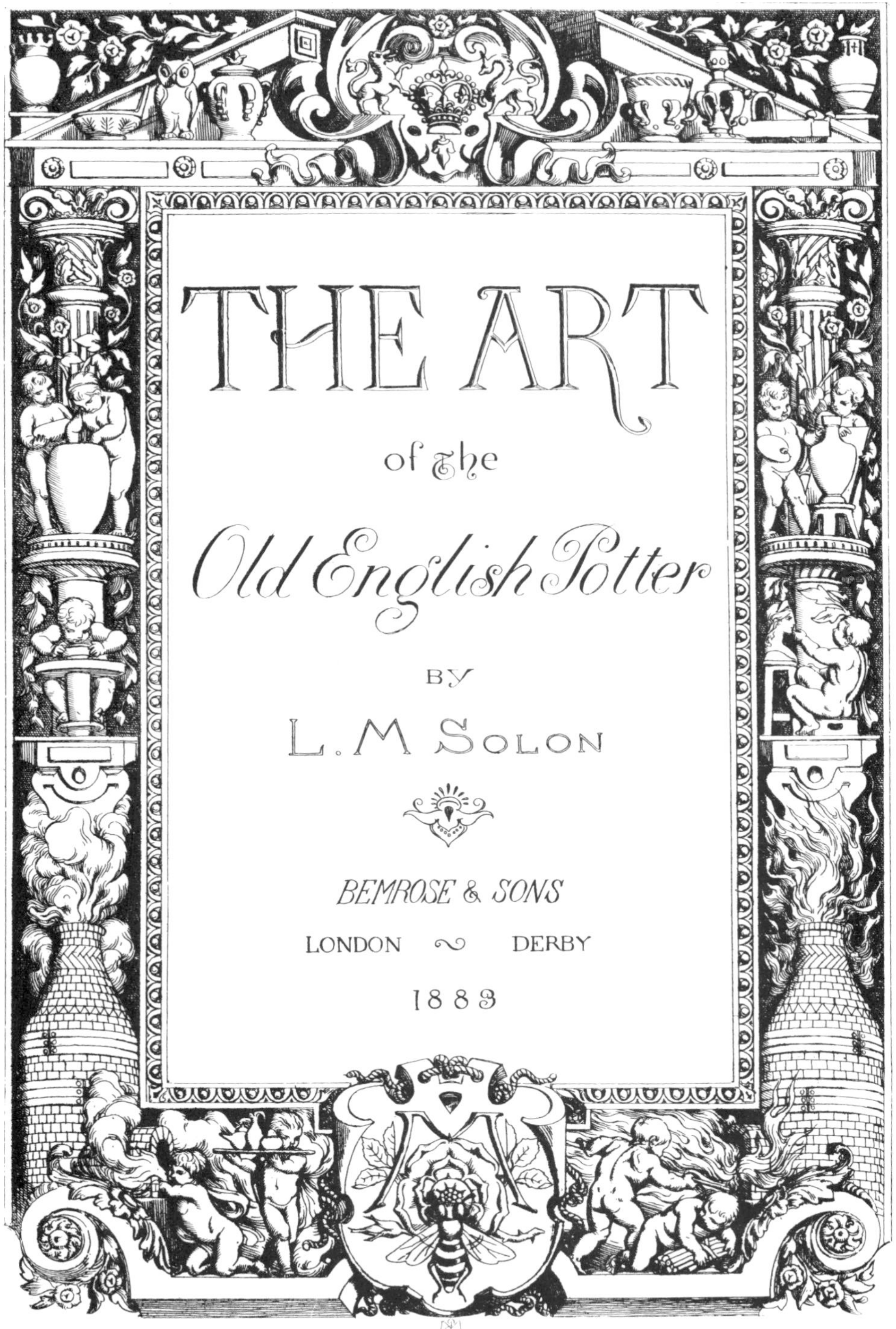
THE ART
of the
Old English Potter
BY
L. M SOLON
BEMROSE & SONS
LONDON ~ DERBY
1883

TO COLIN MINTON CAMPBELL, Esq.

TO WHAT YOU HAVE DONE TO

PROMOTE THE IMPROVEMENT OF POTTERY IN ENGLAND,

THE WORLD AT LARGE WILL BEAR TESTIMONY:

IF THE AUTHOR OF THIS IMPERFECT ESSAY PRESUMES TO DEDICATE IT

TO YOU, IT IS ONLY AS

A TRIBUTE OF PERSONAL RESPECT, AND AN ACKNOWLEDGMENT,

HOWEVER INADEQUATE,

OF MANY FAVOURS RECEIVED AT YOUR HANDS.

PREFACE.

HEN the arduous labour of the week comes to a close, Saturday, in the manufacturing towns of England, brings an afternoon of relaxation welcomed by all. Twelve years ago, arriving from France, having as yet made but few friends, and finding little pleasure besides my work at Mintons', I enjoyed more than anyone that half-holiday, and certainly made the best of it by devoting all the time I could spare to pedestrian excursions, and taking an exhaustive survey of the neighbourhood. Interesting as they were for me, the pleasure of these random rambles would no doubt have soon palled, but just as I was beginning to feel a little weary of going again and again over the same ground without a purpose, an incident happened which created at once an exciting motive for further perambulations. It was the discovery of two earthenware pots, of a kind hitherto quite unknown to me, dimly seen through dusty panes on the window sill of a cottage. Having first asked leave to examine them, I was so struck by their quaintness that I decided to try whether I could not become their possessor. The attempt was successful, the bargain was soon struck, and I proudly carried my treasures home, already considering whether these could not be made the nucleus of a future collection.

Day by day I grew more interested in this strange-looking ware (they were pieces of Salt-glaze), and I resolved to know more about it. Henceforth I could start afresh for the country with a definite aim in view; a new plan was traced, my excursions were to be devoted to the finding and gathering of such specimens of old English ware as destructive time and greedy collectors had so far spared, and might still lie hid in many an ancient homestead. Taking along with me one of those sharp Staffordshire lads whose ready tongue and cool assurance could gain admittance into the most inhospitable dwellings, every Saturday brought about a fresh expedition, and I believe there are few villages, farmhouses, or cottages within fifteen miles of Stoke-on-Trent which, in the end, were left by us unexplored. The excitement was ever on the increase; sometimes at the turning of a lane we came upon a promising thatched house, the old dame to whom the abode belonged often standing on the threshold, and I could faintly distinguish in the shadowy room the ricketty dresser, bearing an array of crocks which, in my imagination, took the shape of so many marvellous and unique specimens that so far had miraculously escaped previous searches, to be reserved for the gratification of the fortunate collector who was just about to secure them. What diplomacy had to be brought to bear before we could obtain permission to investigate the display on the shelves! What a disappointment when all happened to be vulgar and modern; but also what a tremor of expectation when at last the old crone made up her mind to reach from the darkest recess of the corner cupboard the family tea-pot, a modest and yet much valued heirloom, in exchange for which I could offer a price so highly tempting as, in almost every instance, to get the better of family feelings! She then, with a sigh of regret, emptied the contents, generally consisting of a few packets of seeds kept for the following year, the receipt for the rent, and the half-sovereign put by for a rainy day. Remorselessly I bagged my precious find, and retired more eager than ever to proceed on my venture.

Thus old pot-hunting, begun merely as a recreation, waxed into a real mania. The horizon of my expectations kept enlarging every day. No longer satisfied with what chance might bring me, I was bent on finding such rare treasures as visits to museums and the study of books written on the subject had taught me to appreciate and covet, and I entertained distant visions of invaluable *trouvailles.* The huge Slip-decorated dish, ornamented with the stately figures of King and Queen, or rather the abstract conception of what royalty might be, the proud production of one of the common potters of Staffordshire trying his hand at art for the first time, and which, highly prized in its day, never left the dresser it was wont to adorn but on the grand festive days, when it was used to bake the fat goose. The cradle of coarse clay, made on the occasion of the great-grandmother's christening day, and brought on the table for the first time two hundred years before, filled with filberts and walnuts. The traditional tyg, embellished with an unlimited number of handles, and bearing in large letters the name of the possessor. The capacious posset-pot, wherein the compound liquor was brewed at Christmastide only. The lucky shoe, a wedding present, the hob nails of which, made of white slip dots, formed under the sole the name of the owner. The four-handled candlestick, an ornamental article, preserved on the mantel-shelf, together with the most curious belongings of the family, and not the less admired because never used. The white and delicate Salt-glaze ware, stamped or embossed all over with characteristic ornament. The highly-glazed and richly-coloured Tortoiseshell pieces. The Agate-ware, formed of variegated bodies, harmoniously blended. The Cream-colour, so quickly attaining a perfection that has never been surpassed. All these and a host of other varieties were equally exciting my admiration, for in all I could unmistakably trace that freshness of feeling which is so often wanting in the productions of a more refined epoch.

Steadily my collection increased in number, nor did I always keep exactly within the lines I first laid down; shape and decoration were no longer the only recommendation a piece should possess to interest me. This one bore a date which could elucidate a doubtful point; this other, on the contrary, had none, and by that fact became a riddle to unravel; this was precious as being a unique specimen, while the other was a replica of the well-known production of a celebrated maker. In short, I was becoming a thorough collector, and as such began to appreciate anything that possessed historical interest; so it happened that many specimens which at the outset I should have discarded as being of no artistic value, assumed great importance in my eyes.

The object of my pursuits took a definite form. Neglecting the study of all extraneous matter, and ignoring foreign ware and English china, I strove to reach a goal which now distinctly stood before me. I thought of the collection once formed at Burslem by Enoch Wood, and this became the model of what, although circumstances were much altered, and the undertaking was becoming more and more difficult every day, I had to try to emulate. His collection was the only one, I believe, formed with the view of showing the progress of potting in Staffordshire from the 17th century, and it was dispersed after his death. However, one can form an idea of what it was from pieces scattered here and there in museums. It ought never to have left the Potteries. It was divided into four parts, which were sold for one hundred pounds each. One went to the South Kensington Museum; the others were bought by the Jermyn Street Museum, the Mechanics' Institution at Hanley, and Mr. Herbert Minton, who presented his share to Stoke Museum. I must also mention that in his lifetime Enoch Wood sent one hundred and twenty pieces to the King of Saxony.

Brought together as they were, his specimens forcibly exemplified what genuine old English art had been in its pristine days, and one could have derived from them the knowledge that can hardly be gathered now from the stray and rare bits which have come down to us, unclassed and disregarded. It is to be lamented that the early pieces, showing the skill of the first potters, but mostly made for daily use, have shared the doom of all common things in daily use, and are broken and destroyed. It seems as though the English people, whose genius revels in an ever-renewed manifestation of power, whilst hastening to produce a new manufacture, had done its best to make away with all that recalled a beginning of which its present glory made it somewhat ashamed.

And yet, is there anything more interesting for an inquisitive mind than to trace back the progress of an art to its remotest sources; to follow the wandering attempts of its infancy, timid and uncertain, but charming because we are all charmed by everything that is young? Nothing is there in these but what is original and sincere, nothing borrowed from conventional rules misunderstood and ill-applied.

The Greek artist, who by a geometrical tracery originated the symbolical figure of a wave, and placed it at the bottom of a wall or at the foot of a vase, was a creator and a poet; he who came next, and understanding the purport of the work of his predecessor, definitely settled the best use to which it could be put, may be termed a skilful and learned man; but what can we say of the reckless imitator, who, coming at a later period, employs indiscriminately the most commonplace designs of the past, distributing at random figures and ornaments, all dead letters to him, upon any surface, with the sole view of making it gorgeous, and (to take one example out of a thousand) uncoils the symbolic wave of the Greek on the border of a fire-stove? Nothing of the kind is to be found on the works of the potters we propose to study; and we must confess it is chiefly from abhorrence of these out-of-place decorations, often the fruit of a too hasty revival, that we feel attracted towards primitive works, always sound, fresh, and rational. Saturated with sophisticated embellishments, pursued everywhere by ornaments spread on every available space, whether wanted or not, we like to rest our eyes and our mind in looking sympathetically upon the simple attempts of the earliest ceramic artists.

The purpose I had in view when I began to sketch some of my pieces, was to make them known to a few far-away friends, for we all like to draw others into sharing our own tastes, and it is with all of us a pet weakness to discourse and convert. This explains how, by slow degrees, I was led to etch the most interesting specimens of my collection, and subsequently came to think of publication.

If now I venture to write a few words to accompany the etchings, I must, in fairness to myself, say that my ambition never went so far as to attempt a complete history of English Pottery. Others, better qualified than I, have supplied this want; and owing to the assistance of the elaborate and exhaustive books written on the matter, my task has been made comparatively an easy one. It is only in all humility that I venture to present a few observations, suggested by the numerous examples which have passed through my hands, or by the original documents given *in extenso* by the authors who have treated the subject, and to which I shall always refer the reader who may want to know more than he will find in this summary account. But, as frequently happens, examples and documents, instead of settling a question, raise doubtful points or present new problems for solution, I will try in such cases to point out a new ground for controversy, to hazard a probable supposition, leaving the question to be solved by more learned and accurate investigators.

The principal object of this essay will be to relate, as far as it is in my power, the efforts and trials of the first plodders in the field, the unknown ones, who can have no special history of their own, but who, working as a group, made the ground ready for the splendid achievements of the great potters of the latter part of the 18th century.

The discoverers of the early hour are doomed to be absorbed into the commanding individuality of the man who, at the appointed time, arises to condense all their ideas. Setting into shape all that was still rudimentary and unconnected, he appropriates to a definite use all the various processes which up to his time had been little more than so many experiments, and settles the practical rules with which his name will be for ever associated. In this way the fame of the pioneers of the art is eclipsed, their work remains anonymous, and no one cares any more for the names of the forgotten ones, whose combined exertions had such an important share in bringing their craft nearer to perfection. Yet history, which repeats itself, often shows that as long as these early and active labourers are toiling, each of them brings a fresh stone to the edifice; but as soon as the great man, the practical genius, makes his appearance, he seems to erect in the path an insurmountable barrier; he marks the limit, and no one will ever go any further. Like the fruit which completes the growth of some of the eastern plants, he is the sure sign of the coming end; after the fruit has ripened, the plant slowly withers and dies. Retracing the steps of the deviated tradition, to start again from the source will always have a charm for the artist if, by assiduously studying the works of the unknown and the forgotten precursors, he may gather something for which credit may, however tardily, be given where it is due.

This is why we do not intend setting before our readers any specimens of a later date than the middle of the 18th century. The several types it is our purpose to describe are not sufficiently numerous or varied in their fabrication to require a scientific classification; neither is a chronological arrangement called for, seeing that they are comprised within the short period of one hundred and fifty years. In the same way as they are grouped on the shelves of our own collection, we ask permission to present them hereafter. We shall classify them under the following headings:—

EARLY POTTERY—A short retrospective account of the ware which was produced in England before the 17th century.

THE STONE-WARE—Which in the South of England was one of the first attempts at improvement made by the potters, in order to supply the goods hitherto imported from Germany. This object was at last successfully achieved by *Dwight*.

THE SLIP-DECORATED WARE—Or pieces made of the rough marl from the coal measures, ornamented with diluted clay, poured in cursive tracery on the surface, and glazed with "galena."

THE DELFT-WARE—Made in imitation of the Dutch importations; too good an imitation perhaps, as it can hardly be distinguished from the foreign productions, but which, nevertheless, cannot be overlooked, because of its having been extensively manufactured in many places in England.

THE SIGILLATED OR STAMPED WARE—A process probably derived from the German Stone-ware, but which had become thoroughly English when the successors of the *Elers* began to employ clays of different colours, glazing them with "galena."

THE SALT-GLAZE—White and delicately-made Stone-ware, the most English of all in its characteristics, decorated with sharp and quaint embossments, or (but only at a later period) with enamels, and even with printing.

THE TORTOISESHELL—Rich and harmonious, with underglaze colourations, similar in effect to the works of *Palissy*, and of the early potters of the Continent, but differing much from them by the style of the shapes and decorations; and, lastly:

THE CREAM-COLOUR—Beginning with the discovery of the use of flint by *Astbury*, the first step towards the white earthenware which, brought by *Josiah Wedgwood* to the highest degree of perfection, was to supersede all others.

I shall close my account at the coming of the prince of English potters, to whose memory lasting monuments are not wanting—exhaustive books and complete collections. Moreover, his admirable works are so intimately linked to the modest productions of his predecessors, that to write about them is in a manner to make an introduction to the study of his achievements, and indirectly to pay homage to his genius.

By reproducing only specimens taken from my own collection, I thought I should have the advantage of presenting none but examples unpublished so far, and avoiding the representation of what can be seen in public museums. They have been selected out of many, with all possible care and discrimination, to represent the different classes of English pottery. For many years I have spared no trouble in collecting them, and where my own exertions have failed, some kind friend or other has helped me to find the particular piece that was wanting to fill the gap. It is scarcely necessary to say that the study of pieces always before one's eyes is likely to be more thorough than that of examples in public museums, and that it is easier to confer with experts respecting them. Perhaps the amateur who feels desirous of forming a collection of the same sort will be pleased to be shown, instead of what is only to be found in the royal palaces or inaccessible collections, a reproduction of the different types which he may still hope, by perseverance, to discover and acquire.

I shall beg to be excused on these grounds for not having etched any of the choicest specimens I might have borrowed from so many collections, and which, nevertheless, it is my intention to describe to the best of my ability when I have occasion to refer to them, advising the reader at the same time to study them for himself to supplement the shortcomings of my disquisition.

From a visit to the collection which Mr. H. Willett has so generously lent to the town of Brighton, a great amount of information can be derived; nowhere are to be seen so many striking and valuable testimonies to the art of our early potters. A few collectors of taste have not thought it unworthy of their pursuit to secure fine representative examples of old English earthenware, and it is a piece of real good fortune to be permitted to admire the choice selections possessed by Lady Charlotte Schreiber, Dr. Diamond, Professor Church, Mr. Soden Smith, and many others. There is also no lack of interesting pieces to be seen in the public museums, though perhaps justice has not altogether been done there to the productions of the British potter; his little show, selected without much discrimination, and carelessly arranged, stands a poor chance of looking creditable amid the gorgeous display of foreign faïence by which it is surrounded. I must, however, make an exception in favour of the Jermyn Street Museum, which, with its admirable catalogue, forms of itself a complete study.

Before concluding these introductory remarks, it is my duty to cordially thank those to whom I am indebted for assistance in the completion of my book. I am under so many obligations, and my debt of gratitude is so heavy, that I am at a loss to know whom to thank most; I had better confess at once that if there is any interest in what will be found hereafter, the credit is due to others. The greater part of my information I have borrowed from the works of such painstaking explorers in the way of ceramic history as Marryat, Chaffers, Miss Meteyard, Jewitt, and many others. I need not mention their books, for they are so well known. For the formation of my collection, I am indebted to the generosity and unremitting exertions of so many kind friends that I cannot attempt to thank them separately for the possession of the fine specimens which, through their kindness, have passed into my hands.

Last, but not least, I have to acknowledge thankfully the valued assistance received from my old friend Basil Holmes, the painter, and from Mr. J. L. Cherry, of Stafford, who both kindly undertook the revision of these pages; and although I have still to beg that allowances may be made for the shortcomings of a foreigner, I feel less diffident in presenting my incomplete sketch to the reader after it has so much benefited by their careful emendations.

L. SOLON.

STOKE-ON-TRENT, 1883.

CONTENTS.

CHAPTER IV.

ENGLISH DELFT.

CHAPTER V.

THE BROTHERS ELERS AND THE STAMPED WARE.

CHAPTER VI.

SALT-GLAZE.

CHAPTER VII.

EARTHENWARE: CREAM-COLOUR, AGATE-WARE, TORTOISESHELL, ETC.

INDEX

TO THE

DESCRIPTION OF THE PLATES.

CHAPTER I.

EARLY BRITISH POTTERY.

Pre-Historic Urns.—Roman Occupation.—Norman Period.—Mediæval Ware.—Conventual Pottery.—Common Ware of the Middle Ages.—German and Dutch Ware Imported.—Names of the Different Vessels, and their use in the Fourteenth Century.—Tudor and Elizabethan Ware.

EARLY BRITISH POTTERY.

HE opening of the barrows and grave-mounds scattered over Great Britain has yielded a large crop of urns and vessels of the pre-historic period, brought to light in exactly the same condition as they were in many centuries ago. The same explorations have also supplied a few implements of stone or bronze found associated with them. These are the only vestiges that can speak to us of the industry of the first tribes which inhabited the British Isles; they confirm the notion that the Ceramic is as ancient as any art practised by man, but they help very little to unravel the mystery of the epoch to which they belong. They bear no characters or inscriptions of any sort to assist the speculations of the archæologist, while the artist finds comparatively little of interest in their decoration. The shape, simple and rough, such as the hand of the maker can easily produce without the aid of any instrument, is incised or indented with diagonal lines, zig-zags, herring-bones, and punctures, or impressed horizontally by the application to the wet clay of twisted thongs or coarse ropes; but whether termed cinerary urns, incense cups, or drinking vessels, they appear so similar in style that, owing probably to our imperfect education, it becomes a matter of great difficulty to point out any essential difference between the specimens discovered in the United Kingdom, France, or Germany. Sometimes made of well-beaten clay, they are only sun-dried; in other cases they are partially fired. Most of them were put on the funeral pile before being interred with the remains; by this act alone they were calcined;

often the very soil where the cremation took place has been burnt to the consistency of brick. This being observed, must have led to the practice of firing some of the domestic vessels; but judging from the fire-cracks, and the inequality of the burning to be noticed upon almost every example, it is not probable that any kilns or ovens were ever used.

At Trentham, at Stone, in Derbyshire, and all round the district now called "The Potteries," urns and vases of this class have been frequently found, and the modern potter can boast of being able to trace his ancestors very far back into past ages. Important collections have been formed of the ware of the early Britons, such as those of the late Mr. Bateman, Mr. Warne, and others. The British Museum, and the Mayer Museum, at Liverpool, are very rich in curious specimens; their catalogues, and the works of Dr. Birch, Mr. L. Jewitt, and others, contain all the knowledge so far acquired on the subject.

Before the Roman occupation, as we learn from Strabo, the Phœnicians carried on an extensive trade in earthenware with the Cassiterides; so far no evidence has been adduced of the fact, yet we shall here briefly state that we have a bottle of old Phœnician ware, bought in Cyprus, and presented to us by C. M. Campbell, Esq. Its appearance is identical with that of the barrel-shaped bottles given by Mr. Jewitt ("*Ceramics of Great Britain*," Vol. I. p. 88), which present the peculiar feature of the two ends terminating in the shape of a woman's breast. These bottles are said to be English, or at all events to have been discovered in England. Whether this is of any value as evidence corroborative of Strabo, we cannot say with confidence, but we may remark that the shape is not suggestive of British origin.

From the first century to the fourth of our era, the Romans imported into the conquered country the most perfect processes and means used in the Empire; innumerable fragments of red lustrous and other wares are unearthed from every place where they settled, yet they do not seem to have imparted any of their skill to the aboriginal people. Unlike the Gallo-Roman, who, by the side of his conqueror, produced an original style of pottery easily distinguishable, as is attested by the large collection preserved in the Museum of St. Germain, the Briton did not try to emulate the foreign master and to add something of his own to an industry which was not calculated to answer any of his simple wants, so we can hardly trace any real British element in the Anglo-Roman ware, with perhaps an exception in the case of the Upchurch pottery, which appears to show some original characteristics, but there is nothing to tell whether that is due to the particular taste of the first native potter who settled there, or to any external influence.

To follow the transformation of this imported art, which, after having had for a long time a lingering and declining existence, at length revived and developed itself into genuine English pottery, would be too serious an undertaking to attempt here; but it may one day be made evident that one or more of the little pot-works, standing at present in some out-of-the-way spot, has never seen the fire of its kilns extinguished since it was occupied by a Roman potter. What we know for certain is, that the making of a coarse sort of ware has never been discontinued in England. Vessels of burnt clay are of prime necessity to all people, however low in many cases the level of civilisation; and their production is so closely connected with all the arts of fire, in the shape of melting pots or crucibles for smelting metals and glass, and of bricks for ovens and other building purposes, that we need not depend upon the finding of earthen utensils, buried in the soil at different depths according to their age, to corroborate so indisputable a fact.

For us the question to be determined is, At what period did the use of earthen vessels become more general among all classes? Their improvement kept pace with the amelioration in manners and customs, while the plasticity of their material rendered them peculiarly fit to fulfil the increasing requirements of a more refined society; but that it was only late that such a use began to spread extensively may be inferred from the fact of the craft remaining stationary for so long a time.

Of the Norman period we know but little; the manuscripts and tapestries of the epoch give some representations of the pots, basins, and platters then used, but there is nothing to tell us that they were made of clay. On the contrary, old documents mention most frequently drinking cups made of horn, glass, metal, or ashwood; jugs of brass, pewter, or leather; and wooden trenchers. Several rude green-glazed pitchers discovered in Derbyshire have been described as being of Norman make; the horseshoes and the buckles figured upon one of them were considered sufficient to connect it with the Ferrers family, the Norman Earls of Derby; but Mr. C. Gatty, in an interesting lecture given before the Historic Society of Lancashire upon these particular pieces and many others dug out by himself on the very same spot, has forcibly demonstrated that this could not possibly be the case, and he has every reason to believe them to be of a more recent date. Our scanty knowledge of this period is, then, confined to pots and fragments found in excavations; and to these a certain date can with difficulty be affixed.

Towards the middle ages fictile productions began to assume a more ambitious range. The floors of churches and convents were paved with tiles inlaid with clays of various colours, and whereon Gothic ornaments and even subjects of figures were depicted. These tiles present a great variety of processes, being coated with glazes of different colours, embossed and pressed, stamped and sunk, inlaid or painted with white clay. Jugs like those preserved in the Scarborough and Salisbury Museums, and the one found at Lewes, are made in the shape of mounted knights wearing the costume of the 12th century. By comparing these with the knights represented on the tiles of Chertsey Abbey, one might be led to suppose they also had a monastic origin. Tile-making was evidently introduced from Italy and France, where it was practised at a very early period by the monks themselves. Some travelling friars brought it over, and they were very jealous of keeping their professional secrets, applying them only to articles for their own use, whether tiles or such domestic earthenware as was required in the community. A very curious record is found in "*Nichols' Decorative Tiles:*" in 1210, the Abbot of Beaubec, in Normandy, was sentenced to "light penance" for having allowed a monk to work for persons outside the Cistercian order. Here again we find the trade in foreign hands, and the same difficulty besets us to know what share the local potter may have had in the best productions of the mediæval ages.

Meanwhile, the ware turned out of the common potter's oven for homely uses was becoming lower and lower in quality. It consisted of crocks of the commonest description, made with especial regard to cheapness; friable and brittle from being underfired to save fuel, and left porous and pervious. These wares were partially glazed on the outside with brilliantly-hued green, yellow, or brown, to make them look showy in the market place; yet we learn from the "*Liber Albus,*" that as early as 1271 it was ordered that "all earthenware should be well leaded." If ever the potter attempted an out-of-the-way piece whereon to display some unwonted invention, it was in the same way that a country baker occasionally makes a wedding cake. The consequence was that all articles made of clay were discredited, as being vulgar and unfit for any respectable person's use. Down to our own days we have kept something of that prejudice, for he who does not mind showing himself every day with a wooden pipe in his mouth would not care to smoke a clay one in the street.

Only pots of one sort escaped the general contempt; these were the jugs and tankards of German Stoneware, which were often expensively mounted in silver. More than once are they mentioned in the wills of the wealthy; but they were prized merely on account of their rarity, just as the Chinese collector, spoken of by a traveller, valued an English ginger-beer bottle which he had placed amongst his most precious porcelain. So different were they from all that was made in the country that they became an object of great curiosity. We should therefore be cautious before accepting any examples described in the old deeds as throwing any light upon the history of potting in England.

The names of the earthen vessels in use at the time were most of them derived from the French. They are:—

Cruske, Cruskyn, Cruche—A jug.

Crock—Also a jug, often mounted in silver or pewter.

Goddet or *Goddart*—A mug.

Gallipot—A small cup.

Botell, Flagon—A bottle.

Costeril or *Costeret*—A flask to be slung over the shoulder.

Many of these, coloured with mottled glazes, are evidently of French manufacture, and were no doubt brought over by travellers. Others in the shape of a bottle marbled red and yellow were of English make.

Jubbe?—Spoken of by Chaucer.

Just—Holding the exact measure.

Squel, Ecuelle—A shallow basin.

Pitchers—Jugs are still called pichets in Normandy.

Most of these pieces do not bear any decoration; yet the earliest, generally coated with green glaze, are heavily ornamented with embossed heads or rude foliage, the last trace of Roman tradition. At Lincoln, small moulds of terra-cotta were found, together with fragments of the fourteenth century; rude reliefs were pressed separately in these moulds before being applied to the ware. Last year two curious basins, ornamented all round with heads of the same style, were found at Chester; they were used as hand-warmers, and are precisely similar in shape to others dug up in Paris. The journals of the Antiquarian societies of England are filled with accounts of discoveries of this sort. We notice that articles ascribed to the middle ages are, as a rule, very coarse and common. They are jugs, pipkins, piggins, patens or bowls, watering pots, money boxes, children's toys—all articles made for the poor; tygs, dishes, and pieces covered with black glaze are not found amongst the former, being much later in date. These show no longer traces of moulding; the knobs or handles are made by hand, and impressed with the thumb or pinched with two fingers where they join the body. On these common things it is useless to linger, any more than upon the butter pots of Burslem or the garden tiles of Newcastle-under-Lyme, the latter especially not being very much above the bricks of the builder. Far from being, as they have sometimes been supposed to be, the beginning of a revival, we think that they must be considered as the fag-ends of an art fallen into disuse.

Insufficient also are the records of the Tudor and Elizabethan period. Chaffers ("*Marks and Monograms,*" p. 52) quotes many interesting documents. From *Estienne Perlin, Paris,* 1558: "The English drink beer not out of glass, but from earthen pots, the cover and handles made of silver for the rich. The middle class mount them with tin. The poorer sort use beer pots made of wood." From *Harrisson,* 1579: "As for drink, it is generally filled in pots of silver, also in fine Venice glasses of all forms, and for want of these elsewhere in *pots of earth,* of sundry colours and moulds, whereof many are garnished with silver, or at the leastwise with pewter."

But all the pots mounted with silver and pewter, if we may judge from the numerous examples that have come down to us, were no doubt of German or Dutch make. We do not know any instance of an indisputably genuine English jug or tankard associated with an Elizabethan garnish of metal, while there is a large number of foreign ones the setting of which, whether of pewter or silver, is stamped with the English mark.

More to the point are the following quotations, also given by Chaffers:—From the books of the Drapers' Company, 1552, describing the election feast: "There were *green pots* of ale and wine with ashen cups before them." From the Losely MSS. in the sixteenth century: "The gentlemen of the Temple drank out of *green earthen pots* made from a white clay found at Farnham Park."

We must mention, but with a caution, the two brackets preserved in the British Museum. They bear amongst other devices the Tudor Rose and the monogram of Queen Elizabeth, and are richly glazed with green and brown. They are considered of English make, but the style of ornamentation and the quality of the glaze remind one more of the Nuremberg stove slabs than of anything made in England at that time. One of them comes from Hampton Court, and we know that the decorative tiles of that palace were imported from Germany; therefore we feel somewhat doubtful whether these brackets might not have had the same origin.

Nowhere do we find the name of any potter who had attained to eminence, nor does any nobleman of distinction appear to have taken in England, in early times, a special care for the progress of the art by giving his patronage to any earthenware manufactory.

In Italy, *Maestro Giorgio* was everywhere acknowledged as a great artist, and kept at Court equal rank with painters and noblemen. In Germany, *Jacqueline de Baviere* made with her own hands the first pieces of Stone-ware. In France, *Helene*, Countess of *Hangest*, herself superintended the making of the wonderful Oiron Faïence; and later on, King Charles IX. and all his courtiers followed with the greatest interest the labours of *Palissy*. Can we be surprised that the productions of the old English Potter were of so little importance in comparison with what was done on the Continent, when we see how much he lacked encouragement? But times were drawing near when he was readily to answer the first earnest call upon his ingenuity and industry.

Towards the beginning of the 17th century, England seems to have awakened to a feeling of her inferiority, and we find the potter everywhere busy in trying all sorts of improvements, as will be seen in subsequent chapters. If the nobility did not yet require his earthen vessels, the people in their millions were demanding articles appropriate to newly-created wants; the gap between nobleman and commoner was filling up every day in consequence of the social changes which occurred in that century, so between silver plate and rough crusking some gradation was steadily intervening. The man who with a little competence had also acquired a craving for better utensils in his household, could no longer put up with the coarse and plain ale pot of his forefathers; when entertaining his gossip, he liked to see on his table some curious mug which should be a topic of conversation, perhaps an object of envy. With means and leisure came the desire to rival or excel his neighbour's luxuries. Colours and shapes began to be diversified, puzzle jugs of various combinations offered an amusement to the drinker unacquainted with the trick, and the marbled owl became a subject of admiration to all. Tygs (like that in the Mayer collection, dated 1612), candlesticks, and posset pots were designed and potted by spirited artists in a masterly manner, that borrowed nothing from foreign notions. Instead of the shallow colours hitherto employed, the ware was made as white as possible with the Stone-ware body, or of the deepest black with the manganese glaze; ornamentations of different coloured clays were sprigged on the ground, and inscriptions added a special interest to presentation pieces. From this sprang the several branches of English ceramic art, which we shall now try to follow up and study successively.

CHAPTER II.

STONE-WARE.

Stone-Ware and its Glaze.—Importations from Germany.—Mounting in Metal.—Stone-Ware made in England.—Early Patents.—John Dwight and his Discoveries.—Dwight's Porcelain.—The Fulham "Trouvaille."—Beer Bottles.—Francis Place's China.—Nottingham Ware.—Bear Jugs.

STONE-WARE.

HE body of Stone-ware is composed of plastic clay, to which is added some sand to prevent its cracking during the manipulation, and sometimes a small quantity of ground biscuit-ware. Its hardness is due to the high degree of firing it has to undergo, which slightly vitrifies the substance all through. The glaze is a sub-silicate of soda, produced by throwing common sea salt into the oven when the heat has reached its climax; the fumes fixing upon the surface of the ware, and the soda being decomposed, under the action of watery vapours, by the silica of the paste. It is a hard, resisting ware, as its name implies, but not fit to stand any sudden change of temperature; it is very liable to crack or split if put upon the fire, or at the contact of boiling water. So in Germany, where its manufacture originated, it was confined to the making of beer jugs, tankards, or merely ornamental pieces.

From the manufactories established along the Rhine many pieces of Stone-ware found their way into England from the beginning of the 15th century; there, mounted in precious metals, they excited much admiration, and, however rough and common, seem to have been treasured by their possessors. Most of them are of plain brown Stone-ware, with a granulated surface, but a few are of the elaborate white ware made at Siegburg. Some bear the royal arms, and for this reason have been mistaken for genuine English pieces; but in many instances the arms of some German town are blended with the former, which by this fact lose all importance as an indication of origin. The trade extended all over the country; even in Staffordshire common stone grey pots have been exhumed, mixed with early local pitchers, exactly similar to those found in the Rhenish provinces. We believe there is hardly a town in England where there have not been found some of these bottles with a mask on the neck that went by the name of "Bellarmine," or "Greybeard." Although some of them were afterwards made at Fulham, the greater number were certainly of foreign manufacture.

The importation early increased to such an extent that a certain *William Simpson* petitioned Queen Elizabeth, that "he may be granted the only licence to provide transport for the drinking stone pots made at Cologne, which had been so far imported by one *Garnet Tynes*, who is not one of Her Majesty's subjects."

The selling of these pots had become an important branch of home trade, and as early as 1534 the Pewterers' Company had obtained power to stamp their work in the same way as the goldsmiths and silversmiths stamped gold and silver plate. Early German jugs are frequently found with the English pewter mount, stamped inside the lid with the crowned Tudor rose.

The great objection to earthenware had been in early times the porosity of such half-glazed pots as were then provided for common use, and their liability to break when roughly handled; the Stone-ware had neither of these defects; and here again the practical turn of the British spirit is evinced by the readiness with which people of all classes in England appreciated and patronised the hard, resisting ware of Germany, as soon as it made its appearance in this country. The merchants would never have thought of importing the gaudily-enamelled faïence of Italy or France, and no one among the early English potters would have been tempted to imitate them but all could understand the qualities of a new ware so well adapted to their requirements. So while the merchants were bringing over from the banks of the Rhine large supplies of Stone pots, the first efforts of the potters were directed towards finding a home-made substitute for a foreign article so much in demand. It may be that the first factories of Stone-ware were carried on in England with the assistance of workmen brought over from Germany; the trade between the two countries was increasing every day. As German and Dutch potters were commonly coming to England to buy clays and raw materials, it is probable that the facilities the English soil afforded for an enterprise of the kind may have struck them more than once, and induced them to settle here; but at the same time several patents were granted which prove that the national potter did not mean to leave the trade in foreign hands.

William Simpson, above mentioned, after having asked for the sole licence to bring Stone pots into the realm, declares that "in him lieth the power of making such like pottes into some decayed town," but whether he carried that declaration into effect is not known.

In 1626, a patent was granted to *Thomas Rous & Abraham Cullen*, of London, merchants, "Whereas,—heretofore & at the present time, this our Kingdome of England & other our dominions have been served with Stone pottes, Stone jugges, Stone bottelles, out of foreing parts from beyond the seas," a patent was granted to *Rous & Cullen* for having discovered "the art of making Stone pottes," &c., "never formerly used in our Kingdome of England."

In 1636, a patent was granted to *David Ramsey, Esquire*, & others, for, amongst other inventions, "the making of Stone jugs, bottelles, and which now are made by strangers in foreing parts."

In 1671, a patent was also granted to *John Dwight*, "for having discovered the mistery and inventions of the Cologne ware," and also "that he designs to introduce a manufactory of the same ware into our kingdom of England, where they have not hitherto been wrought or made." To this we shall hereafter more fully refer.

Mr. Jewitt *(Ceramic Art of Great Britain)* gives the full text of these interesting patents. We cannot help being struck by the way in which each ignores the previous ones, and we fear that great reliance cannot be placed upon records of inventions that have left so little trace. In the first case it is not difficult to detect a pretence for claiming a sole licence to sell the foreign ware, for which trade a monopoly had not yet been granted. We do not know what exactly to think of the others, but no pieces or "vouchers" that could safely be attributed to these men have ever been identified. As to *John Dwight*, we see that in 1671 he claimed for himself the invention of "the mistery of the Cologne ware," and we have more than sufficient proofs that his works soon competed successfully with those of the foreigners, and even supplanted them in the London market; in fact, the Glass-Sellers' Company contracted with the inventor to buy only of "his English manufacture, and refuse the foreign." To him must be attributed the foundation of an important industry. By his unremitting researches and their practical application, he not only found the means of supplying in large quantities the daily wants of the people with an article superior to anything that had ever been known before, but besides, by the exercise of his refined taste and uncommon skill he raised his craft to a high level; nothing among the masterpieces of Ceramic art of all other countries can excel the beauty of *Dwight's* brown Stone figures, either for design, modelling, or fineness of material.

We know that *John Dwight* established his manufactory at Fulham in 1671. The exact date of his birth has not been ascertained, but his biographers speak of him as having been educated at Oxford, where he was an M.A. of Christ Church, and as having been secretary to two bishops of Chester before he became a potter. Whether he modelled and decorated his works by his own hands is not known through any documents; but by calling any modeller to help him in this respect he would have departed from the custom of the trade of the period. As a rule, the masters then used to perform by themselves the most delicate and difficult parts of their handicraft. Like so many artistic innovators, he appears to have been jealous of his productions, and discontented with the small profit they brought him; at the end of his career he is said to have buried all tools, models, and moulds connected with figure-making, to prevent his descendants reproducing them after his death. In two little books now in the possession of Mr. T. C. Bailey, the present proprietor of the Fulham Works, are contained many receipts and memoranda written in *Dwight's* hand, with dates ranging from 1691 to the year 1695, and following. These are full of interest, but, unfortunately, the wording is often so obscure that little practical information can be derived from them; many of the terms have become obsolete, and besides, some of the mixtures mentioned may have reference as often to unsuccessful trials as to inventions actually accomplished.

For instance, these notes do not, in our opinion, throw any light upon the problematical transparent porcelain believed to have been produced by *Dwight* on the strength of the specification of his patent. If we try to summarise the more likely recipes copied out of his two books, and study their various components, we find that in each case, whether it be "Stone clay for Gorges," "Transparent Porcelain or China clay," "Light Grey clay to endure boiling water," "Grey Porcelain by salt," or any other, we come to the conclusion that these compositions will merely make a good Stone-ware body.

In all cases the principal ingredients are the same; we find the "*best clay*," which is the plastic clay of Dorsetshire; the "*dark clay*," the same probably which is now called black clay, also coming from Dorsetshire; the "*white sand*," always used as a component of Stone-ware; and the "*fine white*," probably a sort of "*frit*," about the composition of which we are left in the dark, and which is made fine by being sifted through the often-mentioned Cyprus sieve.

All the above materials are mixed in numerous combinations, and by altering the respective proportions of each the hardness of the paste is either increased or diminished. With them a good Stone-ware of a whitish or light grey colour could undoubtedly be obtained; but if we look at these mixtures as having any reference to the greatest invention with which *Dwight* has been credited by tradition, we must maintain that none of them can in any way produce a china body, or any other body which in the present acceptation of the word could be called porcelain.

Another explanation may perhaps be given about his invention; we may labour under a misconception of what could be considered, in *Dwight's* time, as a sufficient imitation of the Oriental porcelain to deserve having the same name applied to it. It may have been nothing more than the white Stone-ware, glazed with salt and highly fired; it is transparent in the thinnest parts, and we may assume that Salt-Glazed ware was made so thin for the special purpose of showing some translucency. In *Dwight's* own words, reported by T. Houghton, we have a description of his china, which indicates that a Stone-ware, and not a real porcelain body, was produced. Speaking about the Dorsetshire clay, *Dwight* says, "'Tis the same earth china ware is made of, and 'tis made not by lying long in the earth but in the fire." We need not insist upon the fact that porcelain, as we understand it, cannot be made with Dorsetshire clay. He lays great stress upon the high temperature to which his ovens had to be brought, hoping to succeed by a greater fusibility; but while making all sorts of experiments the probability is that he continued to manufacture his white Stone-ware, trying to make it transparent by casting it thin and firing it hard. We are aware that most of his mixtures required a very high temperature; there is, for instance, in one of the books, a formula for a trial of a china glass (glaze) which could not be melted but at an exceptional degree of heat; besides, from the material with which it is composed, we do not think that this glaze could be suitable for any china body, and this again affords another proof that the intended china was nothing like what we should now call by the name of porcelain.

We can see by the description of his successive trials how much *Dwight's* mind was engrossed by the desire of discovering the secret of the Oriental china; he mentions some specimens he had obtained of a new ware, very transparent, but so fusible that no upright pots but only flat pieces could be made with it. This leads us to surmise that his researches were engaged, like those of some of his contemporaries, in the deceptive track of producing porcelain by way of vitrification; he shared the common mistake of his times, and he could not have succeeded any better than those who had in vain before prosecuted their experiments in following the same delusion.

Some years ago, the attention of collectors was directed to some small jugs of unknown manufacture and strange appearance. With their globular shape and their ribbed necks, they are so much like the Stone pots made at Fulham that by some they were thought to be probably specimens of *Dwight's* porcelain. The paste, somewhat resembling our modern parian, is very transparent, and covered with a good lead glaze. Mr. Willett has been fortunate enough to gather together several of these very rare pieces; they are all clumsily made, and most of them have the appearance of being mere trials; but a small mug of this ware is especially interesting, as showing an imperfect attempt at a coloured decoration, decidedly old English in style, a fact which might weigh against the opinion of some collectors who attribute to them a Chinese origin.

The handle of another small jug now in our collection has been analysed by Professor Church, who found it contained nearly 5 per cent. of soda, a quantity very unusual in any other variety of china. To us it is very doubtful whether these pieces were ever made at Fulham; we do not attach any importance to the shape, which was imitated from German Stone-ware jugs; they may be the work of some unknown English potter, or perhaps essays made on the Continent. At all events, none of the recipes or materials set down in *Dwight's* two books could be conducive to the production of a ware of that sort, and the "mistery of transparent earthenware" still remains a mystery.

The colouring oxides employed on the surface were cobalt and manganese, the purple and blue of the grès de Flandres. The bodies were often tinted in the mass; the blue Stone-ware was coloured with zaffre, the brown Stone with oxide of iron or ochre, and the Red Porcelain was made with Staffordshire clay, probably in imitation of that of the *Elers*. Sometimes the bodies were blended together so as to form a sort of grey and white marble, and then relieved by the application of ornaments made of white clay.

Had it not been for the Fulham "trouvaille" we should still be in the dark as to the precise characteristics of *Dwight's* ware. Twenty-eight pieces, which had been preserved in the family, passed in 1862 into the possession of Mr. Baylis, who at the time wrote an account of them in the "*Art Journal*." Most of *Dwight's* different fabrics are there represented, yet not a single piece of porcelain was found amongst them; a few, like the white ware mug with Hogarth's "Midnight Conversation," the butter boat in the Chelsea style, and the pickle leaves were the works of his successors.

But we are fully enlightened upon the merits of his Stone-ware by the admirable half-length figure (now preserved in the South Kensington Museum) of his infant daughter, Lydia Dwight, who died, as related by the inscription incised at the rear, March 3, 1672; she was modelled after her death, lying on a pillow. We fancy we can trace the loving care of a bereaved father in the reproduction of the features and the minute perfection with which the accessories, such as flowers and lace, are treated. A still more touching memento of the beloved child exists in Mr. Willett's collection; it is her little hand cast from nature, and reproduced in Stone-ware. Beautifully modelled also were the life-size busts of

Charles II., James I., and their Queens. The mythologic figures, in imitation of bronze, were especially remarkable; the Jupiter of the Liverpool Museum is worthy of an Italian artist of the Renaissance; the others, no less interesting, are unfortunately dispersed. Included in the same collection were also some fancy figures of a shepherdess, a sportsman, etc., a few marbled bottles of his Agate-ware, and a blue and white dish bearing the royal arms in the centre, said to have been one of a set made for Charles I.

Another find was made a few years ago, when, in pulling down some old buildings, the workmen came across a vaulted cellar, containing a lot of beer bottles and fragments of jugs painted with the blue and purple grounds generally seen on the grès de Flandres; many were in the shape of Bellarmines or Grey-beards, having the grotesque head impressed on the neck; others were nearly of the same shape, but with plain neck and stamped on the body with crests and badges, a crowned G, Tudor roses, letters, figures of birds and animals, such as cocks and stags, and having reference probably to the inns for which they were manufactured.

This makes the identification of genuine specimens very difficult, for these specimens are very similar to those imported from abroad; both wares are of the same colour, shape, and material, and the decoration is identical, the principal portion being always the portraits or monograms of William and Mary, Queen Anne, George I., and often A.R. (Augustus, Elector of Saxony and King of Poland).

For a long time after *Dwight's* death his descendants continued to manufacture the same sort of jugs and mugs. In cottages along the banks of the Thames have been found many large tankards, bearing the names of well-known public-houses. These tankards are of a particular brown Stone-ware, embossed often with the "Midnight Conversation," or other figure subjects, and always with running dogs or stags; these can safely be ascribed to Fulham. The history of the Fulham factory is related at length by Chaffers, and we learn that it remained in the hands of the family until 1862.

At the Manor House at York, *Francis Place* was experimenting upon clays towards the end of the 17th century; his trial pieces went by the name of porcelain. One of them is preserved in the Jermyn Street Museum; it is a small cup, neatly turned, of brown Stone-ware, streaked with black in the same manner as *Dwight's* Agate-ware. Few other authenticated specimens, if any, are in existence, and the very name of *Place* would, no doubt, have been forgotten by this time, but for a few lines written by Horace Walpole in reference to the above-mentioned cup.

In the Staffordshire Potteries, about 1685, *Miles* and some other potters are said to have made Stone-ware; the probability is that they called by that name a rough sort of brown pottery smeared with lead. As salt-glazing was only introduced a few years afterwards by the *Elers*, the real article cannot have been manufactured before the beginning of the next century; at that time the making of the white Stone-ware, as we shall see in the chapter on Salt-Glaze, became the staple trade of the country, and common utensils were produced in brown ware.

The manufacture of brown Stone-ware became localised in the Midland counties between Nottingham, Chesterfield, and Derby, and so developed itself as almost to exclude every other common sort of earthenware. Pieces made in that district are easily distinguishable from those of Fulham; they affect particular shapes—loving cups, small straight mugs, puzzle jugs, and dark bears; the glaze is very smooth instead of being granulated, lustrous and metallic in appearance, and the decoration, instead of subjects in relief, consists mainly of scrolls, foliage, and flowers, scratched with a point in the wet clay before baking.

At Nottingham, crucibles for glass-makers were made at a very early period, and from this the potters were easily led to the making of Stone-ware. L. Jewitt describes the earliest example known; it is a posset pot dated 1700, made for S. Watkinson, the mayor of the town; it has all the features that characterise a ware which for two centuries has not undergone any alteration in style. The shape is thrown and turned, with handles made by hand; the inscription is in cursive characters, the flowers underneath are only incised in coarse lines, and the glaze is lustred by the remetallisation of the oxide of iron. Many other pieces are known, which are precisely similar as to clay and glaze; the scrolls, rosettes, and the conventional pink flowers are scratched with but little variation; the dates they bear widely differ, ranging from the earliest times down even to our own, and yet they all look as though they had been done by the same hand. Besides the piece mentioned above, dated 1700, we may name the following: in the Bohn collection, a jug inscribed "John Smith, 1712;" in the Jermyn Street Museum, a punch bowl with "Old England for ever, 1750;" in the possession of Mr. Kidd, of Nottingham, a mug very elaborately decorated with roses and thistles, dated 1762; and in our own collection, a puzzle jug of 1799. Neither these, nor the modern jugs and mugs, though ranging together over a period of nearly two hundred years, show any perceptible change either in manufacture or in decoration, and confirm what we have just said on the subject.

A curious speciality of the Stone-ware potters of the Midlands were the black bear jugs. We must confess that they look rather grim and hideous; the body, coated with a very dark brown, is made rough by a sprinkling of small shavings of clay; eyes and teeth are of shining white paste; an iron chain is fastened to the collar, and a staff is fixed between the claws. Such as they were, in that time of bear-baiting they had a great sale, and were used either as tobacco jars or beer jugs; the movable head in the latter case made a convenient cup.

These bears were made at Nottingham, Chesterfield, and Brampton, where originated the making of those ponderous jugs and mugs with handles formed in the shape of a grey-hound, a pattern to which they still adhere in our days, and which is not going to be given up, if we may judge from the large quantity of them still turned out.

We must insist upon the difference that distinguishes the works of the factories just spoken of from those coming from Fulham and the South of England. No doubt the grey and brown Stone-wares were first produced at the latter place, but thence the trade must soon have been carried to such places as presented all the requisites for this fabrication, viz.:—the proper sort of clay, and abundance of coals and salt. The Midland counties afforded all these commodities, and this was certainly known by all the potters of the South, and may have induced some of them to go and settle in such promising spots. Difficult though communication was in those days, there yet must have been a regular intercourse between the potters of widely separated localities. We shall take only the instance of *Dwight* giving in his notebook the recipe for making the red teapots with Staffordshire clay, in the manner of the *Elers*, almost at the same time as the Dutchmen were producing them at Bradwell.

But in the Midland potteries the style of the Stone-ware underwent a thorough change; while in London the Stone pots continued for a long time to be made in imitation of foreign models, greybeards at first, and subsequently globular jugs with royal monograms, it was reserved to the uneducated workmen of these far-away counties to free their productions from alien reminiscences, and to create shapes and decorations which, plain and unpretending as they were, they could yet without question call their own.

The superiority of Stone-ware over every other sort of pottery for the uses of industry, either for utensils or for sanitary works, is so marked that its manufacture has always been on the increase, and the processes constantly improved; but little had been done to turn its merits into an artistic channel since the days of *Dwight*, until *Mr. H. Doulton* created the new style by which the Lambeth ware has become known and admired by the amateurs of Ceramic art all the world over.

CHAPTER III.

SLIP-DECORATED WARE.

The Slip Process.—Its Antiquity.—Its Introduction into England. —Localities where it was Practised.—The Staffordshire Potters.—A Pot Works in the Moorlands.—Dr. Plot's Account.—Reckoning.—Varieties of Shapes.—Names of some Slip Potters.—The Lettering and other sorts of Decoration.—A New Style of Slip Painting.—Richness of Colour. —Metal Mounts.—Inscriptions.— Modern Slip Ware.

SLIP-DECORATED WARE.

HIS process the old English potter, in some sort, made his own by the diversity of effects he contrived to create out of it. It consisted in producing a decoration on the surface of the piece by pouring through a small pipe, clay diluted with water to the consistence of a batter; this slip flowed in running traceries, or dropped in small dots, boldly contrasting with the colour of the ground. The Romans used it very cleverly, and many pieces are still preserved in museums, testifying to the skill with which it was handled. Graceful flowery stems are intermixed with running animals, stags and dogs, whose curved limbs are all produced by the same jet of slip, freely poured through the narrow spout of a vessel contrived to that end. Brougniard mentions the discovery at Lezoux (France) of one of these "pipettes," at the same place where fragments so decorated were found. That "pipette" presented at the lower aperture holes of different shapes, appropriated no doubt to the size of the intended design. A little vessel of almost the same shape was, for the same purpose, used in Staffordshire; to its spout quills of various calibre were fixed; when filled with diluted clay, the air was only admitted into the receptacle through a little hole pierced in the upper part; and the stopping of this hole with the thumb was sufficient to check the flow of the slip. Dots were in that way produced by the intermittent admission of air.

What connection there is between the Roman red ware, ornamented with trailings of white clay, and the oldest Slip-decorated English pieces, if, indeed, there is any, remains to be ascertained. Prior to the middle of the 17th century, we do not find any specimens that we could properly call decorated in that manner. The early tygs, made in the first part of that century, the one for instance in the Liverpool Museum, dated 1612, bear only applications of small pieces of yellow clay, which seem to have been pressed separately in moulds and stuck on. Is there any connection between the English process and the one used in Switzerland and Germany? And was it through Wrotham, in Kent, that it may have passed into Staffordshire? Considering that examples made at Wrotham are somewhat earlier than the dated pieces of Staffordshire, so much might be surmised; but the truth is difficult to ascertain, as pieces undoubtedly anterior to what we possess in England are very scarce on the Continent.

Howbeit, at the date we speak of, we find this fabrication established in many counties. In Kent, it was carried on at Sandwich, where a Dutch potter is known to have settled in 1582; and also at Wrotham, where very elaborate ware was made, including posset pots, dishes, candlesticks, and many different sorts of fanciful jugs and bottles. Although the earliest piece we know (a jug in the Maidstone Museum) refers us only to 1656, many others that can be ascribed to that locality seem by the style of the decoration to belong to an earlier period. Owing probably to the proximity of the Metropolis, the workman there shows a knowledge of the ornaments employed by the artist of the Renaissance on architectural sculptures, carved wood-work, and chased silver. The fleur-de-lys and the pomegranate appear frequently. Stamps taken from metal works began to be used for the decoration of pottery; we possess a terrine, or pie-dish, upon which many subjects of figures, reclining nymphs, and indescribable groups are reproduced, taken evidently from the work of some facetious silversmith of the 16th century. These works are generally distinguishable from those we find in other districts by an overcrowded ornamentation. The handles on the posset pots are multiplied and covered with knobs, and all spaces between the principal subjects are filled in with a diaper of rosettes or stars. A stick, the end of which had been cut as a sort of rough seal, was used to impress the desired pattern in the moist clay.

The manufacture was also carried on in Yorkshire, where, as the traditionary distich has it—

> "At Yearsley there was pancheons made,
> By Willie Wedgwood, that young blade."

In Cheshire, we may infer that the ware was manufactured extensively, from the fact of so many slip dishes having been discovered all over the county, and in North Wales. At the present time, indeed, at Buckley, a few miles from Chester, they have not discontinued the practice of the oldest style, and are turning out slip pieces which, with a little scratching and chipping, might be mistaken for the work of two hundred years ago. Tygs, of course, they are no longer, but the identical shapes now do duty for flower pots.

In Derbyshire, at *Tickenhall*, have been found interesting fragments of pottery, made of buff clay, occasionally streaked with brown Slip; some of them, in the shape of roughly-formed heads, with head-gears and ruffs of the Elizabethan period, seem to indicate that they belong to the 16th century. The potters' field must have occupied at the time a very large area, since fragments have been found there upon a ground extending in length over two miles. Miss Lovell, of Calke Abbey, Derby, who has directed the excavations carried out on the site, has presented to the Jermyn Street Museum some curious tygs and bottles of this ware, selected from the collection she has herself been able to gather together.

The place is mentioned as early as 1630 by Philip Kinder, and later on, in 1811, by Farey *(General View of Derbyshire)*, as being the centre of a very important manufacture of earthen utensils. Slip-decoration followed then the impulse given in the Potteries, as is shown by the two authenticated Tickenhall dishes now in the possession of Mr. W. Bemrose. They are made of the usual buff clay, coated with dark brown, and decorated with subjects of dogs, trees, and flowers, traced in yellow Slip. Many of the Slip dishes commonly known as Toft dishes, had probably the same origin.

But it was in Staffordshire that the Slip process was to become almost a staple trade; there it may be more easily studied; there the old potter has left many records that will permit us to follow his progress. Was he himself the originator, or did he take the hint from one of those itinerant workmen who, at that period, used to begin life by travelling from place to place for a few years, learning a trifle here, and there imparting the small knowledge they had acquired in their travels? Who can tell? At all events, he created a style of his own, where imitation is not discernible. Himself one of the people, he made the ware of the people. No patents were taken out, no secrets were kept; and from one end of the Staffordshire Potteries to the other all ovens soon turned out goods of the same description.

Miserable enough was the condition of the pot makers in Staffordshire, but the district afforded so many advantages for the production of earthenware that it may be easily understood how their number increased rapidly. Clays and coal could be had by merely scratching the soil. The tilewright, a name given to the worker in clay, whether he made tiles, butter pots, or crocks, was at no loss for his materials; and so, notwithstanding the sequestered situation, he soon began to improve his ware, and to find means of sending it away, first over the Midland Counties, and then as far as London.

Miss Meteyard, in her life of *Wedgwood*, gives an interesting and forcible description of a pot-works in the Moorlands in the 17th century. The oven—only one—was eight feet high and six feet wide. It was surrounded by a wall of broken seggars to keep the heat in, and this wall, later on, became the hovel. It stood in a secluded spot, sometimes at the crossing of two roads, near a little stream of water. By the oven, were the thatched cottage and the open sheds, where, clustered together, the different operations necessary to complete each piece were performed. The thrower was in one place; the contrivance he used was of the simplest description, being rather a whirler than a potter's wheel. The potter's wheel is kept in rotation, while the hand that fashions the clay into shape remains fixed; the whirler differs from the wheel in this respect, that one hand turns it at intervals, bringing successively before the other hand the parts that have to be rounded. Next to the thrower sat the handler, sticking on the handles and spouts; what tools he used were certainly very primitive, being nothing more than a bit of iron and a flattened strip of wood. In another shed were, the man who traced upon the best pieces fanciful scrolls and lines of slip, and he who through a coarse cloth dusted upon them the pulverised *galena* for glazing. Very often the same man performed all these different tasks. Close by, the diluted clay was evaporated in the sun-pan, until it became thick enough to be conveniently worked, or else the moistened clay was thrown against a dry wall, where, the water becoming evaporated, the lumps fell upon the ground, ready to be stored in a damp place for further use. Isolated from the rest of the world the potter worked there, attended by his sons and his wife. Sometimes a labourer or two completed the staff, which never seems to have numbered more than eight people. When the stock was ready for sale, the wife took it to the nearest fair, leading, pipe in mouth, the double-panniered asses, and there either sold her goods to the cratemen, or exchanged them at the town shops for such articles as she wanted to take back home.

In his History of Staffordshire, published in 1686, Plot gives a valuable account of the manufacture of pottery at that period. The complete quotation has been given many times, so we shall only recall here its principal features.

Many sorts of clays had already, as we may see, been experimented upon, and their different uses settled, as well as their mixing. Four different kinds were called "throwing" clays, and were used to form the bodies of the vessels. These were the *Bottle-clay* and the *White-clay*, of which the light-coloured ware was made (this was always of a dull yellow colour, for, light as the clay was, the glaze gave it a deep tint); the *Hard Fire* and *Red Blending-clay*, which, mixed together, produced a black ware. Of more pliable nature, and used only for decorative purposes, "to paint with," were the *Orange*, the *White*, and the *Red Slips*, the last named of which turned black under the glaze. All these are easily distinguishable on the works of that period.

The author goes on to tell how the clay was mixed with water in a tank, cleansed from all gravel and other foreign particles, then beaten with a bat, and brought on to the wheel "to be formed as the workmen sees good;" all processes which do not differ much from those practised in our own time. The ware when dry was "slipped or painted." The orange slip made the ground of the ornaments, while the outlines were traced with the dark red slip, studded over with small white dots. In some instances, broad stripes of red and yellow, while still wet, were mixed together with a wire brush, which acted like the comb used for marbling paper or graining wood. Manganese appears to have been the only metallic oxide employed; it was mixed with lead, and "called *magnus* by the workmen." It produced the *motley colour.* As a rule the glaze consisted of the *lead ore (sulphuret of lead)* from the Derbyshire mines, in its native state. When a higher *gloss* was required, lead calcined into powder was dusted over the pieces.

The peculiar way of reckoning the ware ends the description. A unit is said to have been represented by a dozen small pieces, and that unit served as a basis of reckoning for all the rest. For instance, a dish might have been worth a dozen; a very large dish counted for two dozens; of bowls, jugs, cups, and other articles of middle sizes, it required two, three, or four to make a dozen, and so on for all. In that way the potter knew at once the value of the contents of his oven by the number of dozens put in, while the workman could easily calculate his wages by the number of dozens he made in the week. Besides, in the event of any alteration in the prices of the ware having to be made, the unit alone had to be altered, and the scale was modified in all its items. So convenient was this mode of reckoning that, strange as it may appear, it has been kept up to this day in many manufactories, both in England and on the Continent.

Among the Slip-decorated pieces which have come down to us, the shapes are neither numerous nor varied. The potter keeps to a few simple types, all geometrical in their outlines; but these he endlessly varies by decoration, departing in that manner from the taste of his predecessors, who, still under the influence of Gothic art, affected to indulge in natural forms: the representation of a man, or of some heraldic animal. If we find little variety in the shapes of this particular ware, it may be accounted for by the destination of the pieces, which were all intended for mere domestic purposes; and even such exceptional pieces as the workman destined for a handsome present, were made finer and richer by an additional display of Slip-painting.

To mention briefly the different descriptions of earthen utensils most in use at that time, there were: the *Dish*, which we still find in large numbers, and in every variety of size and ornamentation.

The *Tyg*, a tall cup, the simple outline of which was enriched by an unlimited number of handles, always diversified by the fancy of the maker. The *Piggin*, often finely decorated; it is a small round shallow vessel, provided with a long handle at one side for the purpose of ladling out the liquor brewed in the tyg. The *Candlestick*, found most frequently in the south of England, and often adorned, like the tyg, with numerous handles. The *Cradle;* these, on the contrary, are almost peculiar to the Midland counties, being seldom found elsewhere. The *Jug*, including such fanciful pieces as Bears and Owls, and also the *Puzzle Jugs*, on which the number and position of the nozzles show innumerable varieties of combinations. If we add to these a few specimens of very scarce pieces, like *Nests of Cups*, a sort of perforated stand for boiled eggs, *tea-pots*, and *caddies*, we shall have exhausted the list of the shapes upon which the old English Slip Potter displayed his ingenuity.

As through their works the names of greater men in art have come down to posterity, so the few works of the old Staffordshire Potters which have escaped destruction have saved from oblivion the names of several of those modest artists. Why should we not call them artists? In our own estimation they well deserve that name, if we consider how unpropitious to their development was the low condition in which they moved. Some excuse may be found for the roughness of their drawing in the fact that the taste for fine art was only just beginning to dawn upon England; and it is to their credit that they energetically endeavoured to raise themselves above the common level. We must also take into account their insufficient education, and the simple wants they had to supply. Staffordshire was then far from being a wealthy county; what need was there for a more refined ware? The agriculturists and small tradesmen who sparsely populated the district would not readily have chosen goods made more expensive by mere workmanship. The craving for the possession of such articles of luxury had yet to be born in so primitive a community. The few specimens upon which the potter tried to outdo his ordinary work were those he perfected for the gratification of his own pride, or as presents to some friend or patron, to whom he desired to offer an uncommon sample of his skill. Those belonging to that exceptional class all bear witness to that feeling; they are inscribed, "*The best is not too good for you.*" "*This cup I made for you and so no more.*"

In the list of names preserved to us, that of *Thomas Toft* stands first. He was of an old Catholic family, which has still many branches in the Potteries. One of his descendants worked for *Josiah Wedgwood* towards the close of the last century, and had his medallion made at the works at an advanced age. From about 1660, *Thomas Toft* added to the manufacture of usual ware the making of those huge platters the rims of which are ornamented with a trellis-work of orange and brown slip, and the centre adorned with a conventional flower, a nude figure, a lion, or an eagle. No doubt he never thought of deriving his inspiration from nature, but rather from such bits of heraldry, coins, or common effigies of Royal personages as might have come under his notice. He worked in a lane between Shelton and Newcastle-under-Lyme; one of his dishes has been seen at a cottage at Hanley, bearing, besides his name written in slip on the face, this inscription scratched in at the back, "*Thomas Toft, Tinker's Clough.—I made it—166.*." He was probably the first to attempt such an ambitious style as the representation of human figures; many admirers and plagiarists emulated him almost immediately. Whatever the maker's name may have been, most of these dishes seem to have been reproductions, or at least imitations, of one master.

Simeon Shaw *(Chemistry of Pottery)* attributes to *Thomas Toft* the introduction of an "aluminous shale or fire-brick clay," a somewhat obscure specification; but the enumeration Shaw gives of the different improvements by *Toft's* contemporaries shows that he is not much to be relied upon. His information was negligently gathered, and appears to be based mainly on unreliable hearsay. In any case, what we know for certain shows that most of his statements stand in need of corroboration. Amongst the pieces signed by *Thomas Toft* we shall mention: A dish in the Museum of Practical Geology, the centre of which has the crowned lion of the Royal arms, with the usual trellis-work on the border; it is fourteen inches in diameter. One in the Bateman Museum, twenty-two inches in diameter, shows a half-length figure of Charles II., holding a sceptre in each hand. In the South Kensington Museum, a dish, also bearing the full name, has the rude form of a mermaid. Mr. Hulme, of Burslem, possesses one with a conventional flower. In our own collection is another, which represents a Cavalier, his left hand resting on the hilt of his sword, while his right is holding up a drinking glass; it is signed like all the former, and has the same buff-coloured ground and orange ornament traced with a brown line punctured with white dots. We do not know of his ever having signed any cups or tygs.

The name of *Ralph Toft* occurs on several dishes of similar make. One of them, dated 1677, has a figure of a soldier holding a sword in each hand, with a crowned head on a medallion right and left of the principal subject. We find this crowned head very often repeated; we have it on a large dish, where in an arrangement with four fleurs-de-lys, it forms an ornamental rosette; again it appears on another specimen in our own collection on each side of the half-length figure of a queen, inscribed *Ralph oft*, the *t* having evidently been omitted by mistake. In the Salford Museum a *Ralph Toft* dish has, with the name, the date 1676.

John Wright, 1707, from a dish in the Wedgwood Institute, Burslem. *W. Rich, 1702,* (Shaw). *T. Johnson, 1694*, in the collection of the Rev. W. Sibthorpe.

William Sans is mentioned by Chaffers as having also made dishes of similar character.

William Taylor, from a dish in the Bateman Museum, with two full-length figures in the costume of the time of the Stuarts, and from another in our own possession.

George Taylor, with also two full-length figures.

Joseph Glass, of Hanley, whose manufactory was in existence in 1710, and who must have produced a very fine ware of the sort, if we may judge from the beautiful fragments dug up at the place only a few years ago. One of his works is in the collection of the Rev. T. Staniforth; it is a four-handled tyg, bearing *Glass's* name, and the usual Slip designs in brown on a buff ground. Mr. H. Griffiths, of Brighton, has a cradle inscribed *Joseph Glass*, and we should also ascribe to him a remarkably large cradle, of the same style, inscribed William Smith on one side and Martin Smith on the other; at the end a crowned effigy surmounts the date, 1700; this is in our own collection.

Another cradle in our possession has the name of *Ralph Simpson*, and the same name occurs upon a slip dish, with the figures of William and Mary. Not fewer than three *Simpsons* figure in the list of potters established at Burslem in 1710. In this list, drawn up by *Josiah Wedgwood*, and given by Miss Meteyard, many other potters of the time are recorded, but it would be very difficult to identify their respective productions.

Seldom do we find any name on a piece, and if we do find one it generally refers to the person to whom it was dedicated, especially in the cases of tygs, cradles, jugs, etc.

We feel inclined to suppose that if *Thomas Toft* repeated so many times his bold signature on his beautiful dishes, he did it with the view of presenting them to his best customers and patrons, not only as grateful testimonials for past favours, but also as an advertisement likely to bring further orders by the admiration they could not fail to excite. Thus, kept in some country dealer's window as the most conspicuous object in the display, or perhaps set on the dresser of the best room of the house, they remained for long years, becoming heirlooms in the family, until one day, neglected by their possessors, they fell into the hands of the collector.

The broad and quaint Slip letters, acquiring a peculiar shape of their own by the way in which they were poured on, often came in as the main feature of decoration; and we know of many examples where they make a graceful ornament merely by the variety of their lines. Sometimes they are accompanied by huge Elizabethan flowers, very conventional in their shape, and seldom varied in their arrangement; whether brown upon yellow, or light upon the dark colour, they contrast boldly with the ground, and frequently the same piece offers both combinations.

Another process often resorted to is the blending together of red and yellow Slip, in imitation of marble; it is seen on the owls, and on the curious puzzle jug we have reproduced; while again, but in fewer instances, the upper coat of light clay was scratched so as to show the dark ground, in the same manner as the Italian *Sgrafiato*.

Additional portions modelled by hand were sometimes applied. In the Hanley Museum is a jug, dated 1690, which has a figure of Plenty modelled on the front; some thin strips of clay were also laid on and deeply notched with a tool; they have a brilliant effect under the glaze, and constitute another means of decoration also frequently used.

But in no case do we see any moulded or stamped parts side by side with the works of the oldest Slip potters of Staffordshire, as we observe on the Slip pieces of southern origin. They borrowed little indeed from the rest of the world; the absence of oxide of copper upon their early pieces, when we know that all over England that material had been used for centuries, would tend to prove that these worthies confined themselves to their own discoveries. Their pigments were very limited, being confined to the white, yellow, red, and orange Slips. If we occasionally notice a grey Slip on the buff ground, it is due to the discolouration of the orange, through an excess of smoke in the oven.

The traditional manner of employing the Slips never varied, and could not lead to many improvements. The flowers and letters were freely poured on the surface, without any tracing to guide the hand; nor could the process lend itself to much delicacy or elaboration of treatment; yet when stamping and casting began to be introduced, the Slip-decorator found out a way of availing himself of some of the new-fangled methods employed by the more spirited potters working contemporaneously with him. Then we begin to see dishes, the intended decoration of which had been incised and carved on the block upon which they were pressed; thus all the outlines stand out in relief on the piece, and a space is left between the two ridges, forming a receptacle to be filled in by Slips of divers colours. The subjects so treated are much more complicated than those on the usual Slip dishes. We give two specimens of that particular process; and in Mr. Willett's collection is a very remarkable one, illustrating the popular saying, "*A bird in the hand is worth two in the bush.*" In any case the glazing remains the same; it is the rich and lustrous *Galena* unsparingly dusted on, which, liquefied by the firing, spreads upon the piece, if we may say so, like golden treacle. In France the same material was used under the name of *Alquifou.* Though its high colouration forbids its use to any depth on any light ware, it becomes unrivalled when it is intended to varnish a clay already of a dark colour. Few things, indeed, can hold their own by the side of a mellow-toned and richly-glazed Slip piece. We remember once coming across an old Staffordshire dish exhibited in a dealer's window, amidst a host of very handsome "curios," porcelain of all sorts, Oriental silks, and chased silver and gold. The eye that had rested upon the uncouth platter could hardly leave it, and was attracted to it over and over again, so powerful and harmonious did it look amongst all the other treasures. Need we say that we secured it, and were more proud of its possession than if we had been permitted to carry away the most costly of the objects by which it was surrounded?

It is said that in Persia the productions of the most ancient potteries, even though mere fragments, are bought by their admirers at high prices, to be mounted in precious metals with all the skill that the modern workman can command. The same idea was carried out in France in the last century to enhance the beauty of antique Chinese pieces. The coarsest specimens of "Celadon" or "Rouge Flambé" have been set by "*Gouttieres*" and other celebrated chasers in bronzes of the most refined workmanship. In England also this tribute of admiration has been paid by a few collectors of great taste to some of the rough fictile gems of the past; not to speak of the time when the first stone-ware pots used to be elaborately mounted by the silversmith, we know of some instances where a similar sort of setting has been successfully attempted; we regret to say that the examples are only too few in our estimation. The contrast obtained between some roughly made and deeply coloured earthen utensils, mellowed by age, and the sharply detailed and glittering metal work produces an amazing effect.

We have said that inscriptions are one of the main features of old Staffordshire decoration; they are not only interesting in that respect, but also by the humour and sometimes even the pathos which they evince. It is a notorious fact that writing is a prominent constituent of decoration with nations among whom learning has not yet been widely spread. From the Egyptian priests who committed the everlasting evidence of their knowledge to the walls of palaces and temples in symbolic figurations which adepts alone could decipher, to the Moors of Spain, who brought writing into play amongst their intricate arabesques, so as to make of it the more graceful part of the whole tracery, every nation has considered inscriptions, when introduced in their early artistic productions, architectural or ceramic, as answering a twofold purpose, not only to be commemorative of some important event, or memorable date, but also to add another beauty to the general ornamentation. But as the level of education rises in the masses, in the same proportion the letter loses its ornamental character, and its use becomes neglected and obsolete; in fact one might say that inscriptions cease to be employed as a means of decoration at the precise time when everyone is able to understand them. It will, we hope, interest the reader if we give here a few of the inscriptions we have gathered from old pieces of Staffordshire ware.

In our own collection:—

"THE BEST IS NOT TOO GOOD, 1714,"

in brown Slip upon a two-handled and covered posset pot.

"THE GIFT IS SMALL
BUT LOVE IS ALL, 1725,"

scratched in clay upon a brown glazed cradle.

"REMEMBER LOT'S WIFE, 1727,"

upon a yellow dish decorated with brown and red Slip. And several names on tygs, probably the persons to whom they were given:

"MARGRETE COLLEY, 1684."
"JOHN HUGHES, 1690."
"MARY SHIFFILBOTTOM, 1705."

In the Museum of the Somerset Archæological Society:—

"THREE MERRY BOYS, 1697,"

on a nest of cups; the entwined handles are pierced, and allow the liquor to run from one cup to the other.

In the Norwich Museum:—

"COME BROTHER SHALL WE JOIN,
GIVE ME YOUR TWO PENCE HERE IS MINE.
WAYMAN, 1670."

on a brown jug decorated with Slip.

Mentioned by Mr. W. Bemrose in "The Pottery and Porcelain of Derbyshire,"

"GOD BLES THE QUEEN AND PRENCE GORGE
DRINK BE MERY & MARY B B
JOHN MIER MADE THIS CUP 1708."

In the Liverpool Museum:—

"BREAK ME NOT I PRAY IN YOUER HAST
FOR I TO NONE WILL GIVE DESTAST 1651."

In the possession of Sir Ivor B. Guest (see Chaffers' Marks and Monograms):—

"COME GOOD WOMAN DRINK OF THE BEST
YOU MY LADY AND ALL THE REST."

upon a brown four-handled tyg.

In Mr. H. Willett's collection, Brighton:—

"ANN DRAPER THIS CUP I MADE FOR YOU & SO NO MORE.—J. W., 1707."

upon a brown and yellow posset pot.

"THE RIT GENURAL CORNAL FOR THE DROWNKEN REGIMENT,"

on a large beer jug.

The alphabet in square compartments and the date, "*May the 29 Day, 1706*," on a large posset pot.

In the British Museum:—

"REMEMBER THY END TRULY,"

upon a pot of questionable shape.

Specimens of what we might call "speaking pottery" are somewhat limited in number, as the style is confined to presentation pieces, sacredly preserved in old families. They were so difficult to obtain that we do not find any in the collection of Enoch Wood, who yet had shown himself so zealous in collecting all that could be interesting for the history of the old Staffordshire ware; but he was probably unable to secure any.

During the latter part of the last century the art of Slip was superseded by more advanced processes of decoration; however, in the Liverpool Museum is a brown puzzle jug bearing a long inscription, very neatly poured on, bearing the date 1828. At the present day, in the market places of Norfolk, Kent, and Lancashire, we meet with coarse pots and pancheons which are streaked here and there with lines and scrolls of white Slip, made in some remote country pot works. In Switzerland the tradition is still kept up, though it has lost many of its ancient characteristics, and the peasant's ware continues to be made pleasant and gaudy by the use of different coloured clays poured on the ground in the same manner as of old.

In Italy, also, a ware of the same sort is extensively fabricated, and it requires a very skilful hand to dash on at one stroke, with the liquid Slip, the conventional flowers and animals that suit the taste of the people. A Milan manufacturer having engaged for that special work a pastry cook, who was extremely clever at embellishing his cakes with designs in syrups and currants, has found his talents so successful when thus directed to pot painting, and his work meet with such a demand, that he realises more profit out of the extemporised artist than he would out of half-a-dozen china painters.

May we be excused if we show ourselves a little partial to the Slip process, considering that it is closely connected with "*Pâte sur Pâte*," a process that we have practised ourselves for more than twenty-five years, and which is also painting in Slip upon the unbaked surface?

We shall conclude by mentioning another sort of Slip-ware also made now-a-days, the sham "old Slip," of which we have to confess the possession of several pieces, bought at a high figure for genuine specimens. We wish our experience to be of some use to other collectors, and hope our readers may be spared the disappointment of finding that a piece bought in a lonely cottage from a respectable-looking old woman, turns out to be nothing but an impudent forgery! "Forewarned, forearmed."

CHAPTER IV.

ENGLISH DELFT.

DUTCH-WARE.—ITS BODY AND GLAZE.—DELFT MADE IN ENGLAND—LAMBETH—LIVERPOOL—BRISTOL—THE STAFFORDSHIRE POTTERIES.—ENGLISH DELFT DISHES.—UNSUCCESSFUL ATTEMPTS TO MANUFACTURE DELFT IN THE POTTERIES.—INSCRIPTIONS.—ENGLISH DELFT ONLY MADE AS AN IMITATION OF FOREIGN WARE.

ENGLISH DELFT.

ROM Holland, where factories of the white ware coated with stanniferous enamel had been in existence from an early date, the process was brought into England about the middle of the 17th century. It was the nearest approach to the Oriental porcelain, which was so much admired, and so difficult to obtain. The Dutch, who imported it from the West Indies, endeavoured to transform into a plausible substitute the common white faïence they were then making, and by decorating it in blue with subjects copied from Chinese pieces, to realise, if not the unobtainable transparence, at least all the outward looks of the Eastern China. They succeeded in producing such a close imitation that some of the blue and white Delft dishes might, at a distance, deceive the eye of even a connoisseur.

The body is of a yellowish or red colour, very friable and porous; carbonate of lime enters largely into its composition. The glaze, a thick and opaque enamel, is a mixture of oxides of lead and tin. Its manufacture differed from all other early ware in this respect, that it had to be fired twice; once to harden the biscuit, so as to allow of its being dipped in the liquid glaze, the porosity of the body absorbing the water while the enamel remained on the surface; and then a second time to vitrify the glaze.

The earliest dated pieces considered to be English Delft, that is to say, potted in England, were probably made with clay from Holland, as we may infer from the fact of their substance being very porous, and easy to cut into with a knife; from its effervescing with nitric acid, and at a high temperature melting into a coarse glass. The native clays, however, were soon brought into use, and then we find the ware has been highly fired, and can hardly be scratched with a sharp blade. It is of some importance to remark that the list of all the British clays drawn up by Mr. Maw, and published in the catalogue of the Jermyn Street Museum, does not contain any calcareous clay like that which constitutes the principal element of the foreign stanniferous faïence. However, the ware was made in England with the local materials, only the biscuit being dense instead of spongy does not when dipped retain a sufficiently thick coating of enamel, and its red colour shows through, giving to the ware that rosy tint so often observed by collectors; crazing is always seen on the surface through want of affinity between body and glaze. Dutch pieces, on the contrary, are as a rule free from this defect. The English potter was so well aware of this shortcoming that the early dishes were coated only on the front side, the back being glazed with the usual lead glaze, and sometimes mottled with ordinary tortoiseshell colours. Whenever the style of painting, which otherwise is the safest guide for identification, appears doubtful, this should be sufficient to indicate the origin of a piece. Dutch dishes may be found similar in design, but they are invariably enamelled on both sides; as to the few dishes of Italian make which possess the same peculiarity of being glazed with lead on the back, their decoration is so characteristic that in their case a mistake is almost impossible.

This white and painted earthenware was made in or near London, towards 1668, as appears from the record of a lawsuit instituted by one *Edmund Warner* against the Custom House authorities, who had seized one of the parcels of potters' clay which he used to import from Holland. The trial took place in 1693, and five London potters gave evidence as to the clay being of the kind they had constantly bought from the said Warner for above 25 years. (Catalogue of the Museum of Practical Geology, p. 300. Appendix.)

At the date of 1676 a patent was taken out by *John Arien Von Hamme*, for the sole practise of "the art of making tiles, porcelain, and other earthenware, after the way practised in Holland, which has not been practised in this our kingdom." It would be difficult to reconcile this pretension with the fact that many pieces bearing an unmistakably English stamp are found inscribed with a much earlier date. Thus a Delft-ware mug in the Jermyn Street Museum is dated 1631, and inscribed "*William & Elizabeth Burges;*" another in Mr. Willett's possession is painted with the name of "*John Leman, 1634.*" One may assume that towards the same period English-made tiles were extensively in use for interior decoration. Bottles of Delft-ware were commonly used to keep foreign wines in; they were all dated in blue pencilling to record the year in which the wine had been bottled. We find them with "Sack, 1649," "Claret, 1648," "Whit, 1648," &c. One of a larger size, in the Norwich Museum, has the Grocers' Arms, the monogram W / E M E, and the date, 1649. None has been found to be dated later than 1659.

Sets of three or four cups, with their handles entwined (an essentially English shape), were made in Delft as well as in Slip-ware. A mug in the South Kensington Museum is inscribed "*Ann Chapman*, 1649." Many pieces bear the arms of the City Companies. Mr. A. Franks has one with the arms of the Bakers' Company, 1657, and another with the Leathersellers', 1660. In the Bohn collection was a quaint-shaped cup, with the portrait of Charles II., and the motto, "*Be merry and wise, 1660.*" A cup in Professor Church's collection had "*God save the King, 1662,*" inscribed under a crown. We possess a cup, with twisted handle, with the monogram R / A I disposed in the English manner, the top letter standing for the surname, and the other two for the Christian name of the husband and wife, and the date, 1667; also a caudle pot with three letters and 1687.

Drug pots, inscribed in English with the name of their contents, and pill-slabs, may also be ascribed to Lambeth. The production of English Delft became very important in that locality, for it is said that at one time twenty factories were occupied in making it. Though it never became general in England, the manufacture was established in some of the seaports which had a regular trade with Holland. At Liverpool it was for a time the "principal trade of the town," according to the Holt & Gregson MSS., quoted by Mr. Charles T. Gatty, from whom we borrow the following extracts:—"To stone building (1660) there succeeded brick and slate building in Liverpool. To brick making succeeded the clay potteries. To them Delft-ware.

To the Delft-ware succeeded the whole flint or Queen-ware in 1760, by *Wedgwood.* The Delft-ware every merchant of note in Liverpool was concerned in early in the 18th century." The progression in the different branches of the trade is plainly described, yet in this case also pieces authenticated by tradition carry us back to a still earlier period. A Delft mug in the Liverpool Museum, attributed to Liverpool manufacture, is inscribed "*John Williamson, 1645.*" If we can implicitly trust its evidence, the ware had been manufactured long before the period referred to by the writer.

In 1716 the English Delft had already been brought near to perfection, as we can see by the large plaque preserved in the Mayer Museum; it is painted in blue, with a view of Great Crosby, the landscape being plentifully diversified with ships, houses, figures, and animals of all sorts. In the old church at Crosby may also be seen a plaque of the same ware, with the arms of the Merchant Taylors' Company, and the date, 1722. At that time the ware was already exported in large quantities, and numberless examples have been preserved to us dating far down in the 18th century. Among these may be mentioned tiles for fire places, with blue landscapes and figure subjects; puzzle jugs of elegant shape, thinly potted and brightly glazed, with doggrel verses painted all round; and especially large punch bowls, decorated with a ship in full sail and a border of Chinese flowers. On these the blue painting is so cleverly executed that they vie with any piece made in Holland, and the artists had nothing more to learn from their masters. *Shaw* and *Pennington* were very celebrated for their punch bowls between 1750 and 1780. The Mayer Museum has one 17½ inches in diameter. Another of the same style in the Jermyn Street Museum is 20½ inches in diameter. In the Mechanics' Institution at Hanley, another bowl, also 20½ inches in diameter, is rendered particularly interesting by the label accompanying it, which has been written by the painter himself: "*John Robinson, a pot painter, served his time at Pennington's, in Shaw's Brow, and there painted this punch bowl.*" They are all of them masterpieces of the craft.

At Vauxhall and Mortlake, Delft-ware potteries were carried on, but no specimens have been so far identified as coming from these places.

At Bristol, English Delft was extensively manufactured from the beginning of the 18th century, but the potters of that city never attained to the degree of perfection which the art reached at Liverpool. The glaze is far from being so bright, and some of the colours are dull, and lack the gloss usually noticed in the fine stanniferous enamel. A plate painted in blue, dated 1703, and a high-heeled shoe, dated 1722, are referred to Bristol manufacture. Tiles for house decoration were painted, so as to form, when put together, a large panel. Thus the Jermyn Street Museum has a set made at *Richard Franks'*, 1738—1750, upon which is painted a view of Redcliff Church. Mr. Fry has two sets of nine tiles each, with the picture of a cat and a dog, and Mr. Willett a copy of Hogarth's "March to Finchley," on a panel composed of seventy-two tiles.

Thomas Heath introduced Delft-ware into Staffordshire. *Shaw* tells us how he contrived a new mixture of clays from the coal measures. He describes a dish made by this potter, "which was one of a set manufactured as specimens of that new kind of ware." Though the author mistakes the white enamel for a dip of white clay, the description is so accurate, that there can be no doubt as to the piece being English Delft. "The upper surface is tolerably even; but the under surface is spotted with minute holes, and exhibits the coarse material of the body." The same peculiarity is to be noticed upon the back of nearly all the dishes coming from Holland; the cause is, that while the inside of the dish is formed upon a mould, with a bat of clay carefully smoothed on the surface, the outside has to be cut and turned, thereby exposing all the small holes that may exist in the bulk of the clay; and as the glaze does not penetrate them, after the firing these perforations remain and are increased in size. This was considered such a drawback by the Staffordshire potters that, as we have already observed, they did not attempt to enamel the backs of their dishes, but merely glazed them with lead. In that manner are made those huge dishes representing Adam and Eve under the tree of knowledge, King William and Queen Mary, Queen Anne, George I., and many celebrated personages of the time. The style of painting is not very commendable; the figures are rudely drawn, and heavily patched with blue; sometimes there is a random staining of copper green or a few dashes of yellow, and clouds and trees are daubed on with a rag or a sponge soaked in blue. It seems as though the painter, whose unattractive task was only to follow a foreign model, did not care whether he pleased himself or anybody else. The rims are marked all round with heavy strokes of the brush, in a way that recalls the indentations practised on the edges of the Slip dishes.

This new kind of ware was no doubt very successful, and its production was stimulated by the serious competition the Dutch carried on against the English potters, even upon their own grounds. The dishes representing William and Mary were first made at Lambeth, before being imitated in Staffordshire. William III. seems to have fostered by all the means in his power the introduction into England of the faïence of his own country. He was wont to make presents of his portrait painted on large dishes; and it was at the suggestion of his ambassador at the Hague, that A. Von Hamme came over to establish a factory in London. In an old family at Dartmouth is still preserved one of these dishes, which the king himself gave to one of the ancestors, then mayor of the town, in acknowledgment of services rendered when he landed as Prince of Orange.

Delft-ware became so fashionable that the English potters had to apply that name to such substitutes as they could contrive to manufacture. The ware has disappeared a long time ago, but the name has been preserved to this day, and all common crockery is still called *Delf* in many country places. Lane-Delf became the name of the place where stood the several potworks manufacturing it, but not before the end of the 17th century, as it is not marked on the map drawn by Dr. Plot. It was situated between Lane End and Fenton, and at the present time forms part of the last-named town.

Earnest efforts were made to naturalise the stanniferous enamel in the Potteries, but with little success, the result being very unsatisfactory. The glaze is poor and crazes badly; the colours do not approach the liveliness of continental faïence; besides cobalt and manganese, mostly used, we see only copper green and antimony yellow sparingly employed, and without any brilliancy. The process was hardly diversified in its effects. We possess two jugs coated with a stanniferous blue, decorated with white enamel, much in the style of the Nevers' faïence, and a teapot which has the same opaque ground, combined with transparent enamels, and fired in the Salt-glaze oven; but specimens of these kinds are seldom met with.

Not only was the ware ill adapted to domestic requirements, but the tin so largely used in its manufacture was so expensive a material that the potters had to tax their ingenuity until they could supply a somewhat similar article more easily and cheaply manufactured. The white dip, invented by *Astbury*, was resorted to, and might have been successful in its application but for the imperfections of the lead glaze, which tinted it deeply with yellow. Nevertheless the regular earthenware was found so much superior in quality, that in the Potteries the attempts to imitate the foreign Delft were soon abandoned, while dipped or cream-colour ware, painted in blue, continued to go by the name of *Delf*. The "dip" process, that is to say, the coating of a coarse clay with a fine white one, was still in use at the beginning of the present century; many of the best blue printed dinner services, with Chinese patterns, are made in that way; the breaking of a piece exhibits a coarse body covered with a thin layer of white slip.

Upon the pieces of Lambeth, Liverpool, and Bristol manufacture inscriptions occur frequently, and although they lack the "naïve" simplicity of the slip ones, many of them are well worth being recorded. They take the form of short mottoes on the earliest pieces:—

"MAY IT BE WELL USED."

"BE MERRY AND WISE."

On shaving dishes:—

"YOUR QUARTER IS DUE."

On a small caudle pot, as a wish:—

"BOY."

Later on we find allusions to political events:—

"PARLIAMENT BOWL FREE WITHOUT EXCISE, 1736," and

"GOD GRANT UNITY, 1746."

Upon six dessert plates, each having one line of a verse, we read:—

1. "WHAT IS A MERRY MAN?"
2. "LET HIM DO WHAT HE CAN,"
3. "TO ENTERTAIN HIS GUESTS"
4. "WITH WINE AND MERRY JESTS,"
5. "BUT IF HIS WIFE DO FROWN,"
6. "ALL MERRIMENT GOES DOWN—1738."

On a bowl in the Geological Museum:—

"JOHN UDY OF LUXILLIAN
HIS TIN WAS SO FINE
IT GLIDERD THIS PUNCH BOWL
AND MADE IT TO SHINE, &c., &c.—1731."

"ONE BOWL MORE AND THEN."

Doggrel verses, all to the same purport, are very varied on the puzzle jugs:—

"HERE GENTLEMEN COME TRY YOUR SKILL
I'L HOULD A WAGER IF YOU WILL
THAT YOU DON'T DRINK THIS LIQUOR ALL
WITHOUT YOU SPILL OR LET SOME FALL."

"FROM MOTHER EARTH I TOOK MY BIRTH
THEN FORMD A JUG BY MAN
AND NOW STAND HERE, FILLD WITH GOOD CHEER
TASTE OF ME IF YOU CAN."

"IF THIS BE YE FIRST THAT YOU HAVE SEEN
I'LL LAY THE WEAGER WHICH YOU PLEASE TO PAY
THAT YOU DON'T DRINK THIS LIQUOR ALL
WITHOUT YOU SPILL OR LET SOME FALL."

"WITHIN THIS CAN THERE IS GOOD LIQUOR
'TIS FIT FOR PARSON OR FOR VICAR
BUT HOW TO DRINK AND NOT TO SPILL
WILL TRY THE UTMOST OF YOUR SKILL."

This is an example of friendly inscriptions on presentation pieces:—

"JOSEPH SWADELL.
WHEN THIS YOU SEE REMEMBER ME
AND BEAR ME IN YOUR MIND
LET ALL THE WORLD SAY WHAT THEY WILL
SPEAK OF ME AS YOU FIND.—1774."

We might multiply quotations, but the above will suffice to show that the Delft potter was very prolific in his poetical lucubrations.

So many counterfeits of foreign ware were made in England as to compel us to acknowledge that, as a rule, English potters were in many instances not over scrupulous as to the way in which they tried to palm off their productions as something different from what they really were. Thus Stone-ware and faïence were at first styled Porcelain; at the same time that English ware was made to imitate foreign, the latter was sold as home-made. It is also well known that no sooner did some ingenious potter originate a new process or style, and endeavoured to protect it by affixing his mark, than these marks were pirated in a shameless manner. Were it not that English Delft had its halcyon days which cannot be ignored, this chapter ought never to have been written for a book whose special purpose is to point out what was original in the early Ceramic Art of England. In some cases, out of a mere imitation a particular style may develop itself; by degrees it frees itself from leading strings, and then runs freely on a new course; but it was not so with the tin-glazed ware of British manufacture; never was it raised to a very high level, nor did it even attempt to leave the track of a spiritless imitation. The best Liverpool pieces are nothing after all but copies of the Dutch faïence, and would be indistinguishable from their models but for the English inscriptions and a certain clumsiness of execution. Those who manufactured them have left their names in many documents of the time, but by no means the impress of individual genius upon their works; nor did they bequeath the least discovery or improvement for which any credit can be given to them.

CHAPTER V.

THE BROTHERS ELERS AND THE STAMPED WARE.

THE BROTHERS ELERS COME FROM HOLLAND.—SOME ACCOUNT OF THEIR FAMILY.—JOHN PHILIP PROBABLY THE POTTER OF THE TWO. —BRADWELL WOOD AND DIMSDALE.—THE RED WARE.—METAL DIES USED TO STAMP THE ORNAMENTS.—BLACK WARE.—THE IMITATIONS.—TESTS FOR IDENTIFICATION.—THE WORD PORCELAIN APPLIED IN THAT TIME TO OPAQUE WARE.—INTRODUCTION OF SALT GLAZING.—DEEP SECRECY PRESERVED IN THE MANUFACTORY.—ASTBURY AND TWYFORD DISCOVER THE SECRETS.—THE ELERS LEAVE STAFFORDSHIRE.—JOHN PHILIP JOINS THE CHELSEA GLASS-WORKS. — HE SETTLES IN DUBLIN.—THE WORKS OF ASTBURY AND OTHER IMITATORS.—PORTOBELLO WARE.

THE ELERS.

HAT the Moors of Spain effected for the improvement of the potter's art in Italy, and what subsequently the Italians did in France (as it has now been ascertained), for the introduction of a new kind of pottery, which was to develop itself there into so many varieties, the Brothers *Elers* did for the advancement of earthenware in Staffordshire. The uneducated butter-pot makers and tilewrights were just beginning to feel the first stirrings of an ambition to improve their coarse productions, when the *Elers* came among them, bringing new ways and new tools, and above all, a taste for beauty and refinement, a feeling hitherto unknown in the district, but which was to give an impetus to the latent desire for perfection, without impairing the native originality.

From Holland the Brothers *Elers* seem to have followed the fortunes of the Prince of Orange, and to have come in his train to England in 1688. They were of a noble family of Saxony. Mr. Jewitt *(Life of Josiah Wedgwood)* gives their complete genealogy, but it will be sufficient for our purpose to relate that their father had been Ambassador to several courts of Europe, and that during his term of office as Burgomaster of Amsterdam, he is said to have harboured in his house the royal exile, Henrietta Maria. , His two sons, our potters, were John Philip and David; the Elector of Mentz and Queen Christina stood godfather and godmother to the former.

The date of their arrival in Staffordshire is somewhat uncertain; nor is it known whether William III. continued to extend his patronage to them beyond granting a pension of £300 to their sister. David set up as a merchant in London. Was it in the course of his business transactions that he became acquainted with the peculiar advantages offered by Staffordshire for the establishment of a potting manufactory, and that the brothers decided to settle on the spot? Or, rather, was it that on coming to England they at once sought the acquaintance of *Dwight*, then the leading man of the trade, and himself of Dutch extraction, and in this matter did they act on his advice? *Dwight*, during his stay in Chester, had experimented upon all the clays of the neighbourhood, and no one more likely than he could have directed their attention to the remote spot on which they ultimately settled. In 1698 they had already been long at work. Dr. Martin Lister speaks about the red-ware made "by the two Dutchmen brothers who wrought in Staffordshire, and were not long since at Hammersmith." From this we may infer that they were occasionally together in London; but it is probable that while David was selling the ware at his shop in the "Poultry," John Philip was manufacturing it at Bradwell Wood. Indeed when his son, *Paul Elers*, writes to *Wedgwood* in 1777 about his father, he seems to claim for him alone the honour of having been the first potter in England, directing that under his portrait should be engraved "*Johannes Philipus Elers, Plastices Britannicæ Inventor*" (Miss Meteyard, "*Life of Wedgwood*").

Bradwell Wood is at the present day as lonely a spot as it was in the time of the *Elers*. It lies some distance from the road leading from Wolstanton to Burslem, and a farm-house is the only building on the place. Dimsdale, where the *Elers* stored and sold their productions, is about a mile distant. It is a timbered building of the Elizabethan period, half manor, half farm-house. It has a small pool of water in front, and clumps of old trees encircle it. In the interior a very dilapidated wainscoted room is all that remains of what may have been in the past a noble building; and in that case, if they did really inhabit the hall, the aristocratic potters found there a home befitting their station. At this moment, when the newly-discovered telephone is used so extensively, it is curious to recall the story that the two places had been connected together for convenience sake by a speaking tube made of clay pipes, through which a conversation could be carried on.

There, ready to hand, was to be procured the red clay they wanted for their best work, the ware which at that time went by the name of red porcelain, and was to be the first step towards the imitation of Oriental hard pottery, "for which," says Shaw, "they mixed one part of the Bradwell red clay and four parts of the Hill Top clay." Numbers of hands already trained to the common drudgery of potting were also available on the spot. No doubt this was of great assistance to the new comers, and yet we shall see further on how much they distrusted such helpers as they were obliged to employ.

The *Elers* red-ware is a dense and semi-vitrified body, which chemically differs only from porcelain by its lack of translucency. Professor Church gives its hardness as about 5 on the mineralogical scale, and its density as ranging between 2·3 and 2·41. The fineness of the paste is due to the careful levigating and sifting of the natural clay, and its hardness to the high degree of firing to which it was submitted. The colour of the body is of a lighter tint than that of the red-ware made by other makers, and the pieces are especially remarkable for the neat and skilful way in which they were turned on the lathe. Very peculiar is their style of ornamentation. Simple though it is, it can be said to have little resemblance to anything done before. It was derived from the recollection of some Japanese or Chinese pieces, imitated, but not actually copied, and so it became a style of its own. Rigorous reproduction was certainly not the aim the *Elers* had in view when they produced their red teapots, which had nothing Oriental in them but their outward look, for they did not use any of the means which would have conduced to a close imitation, not even the pressing and moulding which were always employed by the Chinese for those pieces which are regarded as having been their models. The raised designs that slightly decorate the smooth ground were obtained by means of small metal dies sunk in the shape of a flower or a leaf. On the surface, delicately lined over and finished on the wheel, a little lump of wet clay was applied and stamped in the same way as the impression of a seal is taken upon wax. The excess of clay round the outlines was then carefully scraped off with a tool, and the flowers and leaves were connected together with stems made by hand, so that with the same tools the pattern might be greatly varied. The impressions sometimes represent small figures bearing a strong German character in their design. Thus we have: the four quarters of the globe; a lady holding a flower, or a huntsman with his gun; but most frequently the ornamentation consists of rosettes, scrolls, or "entrelacs," quite typical in their arrangement. The handles and spouts are plain, and were made by hand. The articles made by the *Elers* were very simple, and, so far as we know, restricted to tea-ware. We never came across a single piece of red-ware which was merely ornamental, and which could at the same time with certainty be ascribed to them.

Though stamping on clay had been commonly used centuries before, on the Samian ware for instance, which was also made of fine red clay, well turned and impressed with seals, on the German grès Stone-ware, and even upon some early English pieces; yet the *Elers'* way of using the tools was very different, and the effect does not recall to the mind any of the above-mentioned potteries. In the Hanley Museum are still preserved a few of these dies, and also some brass moulds in use at the same period for making spoons and other small pieces.

A black body made from a mixture of "red clay and oxide of iron," and probably manganese, is said to have been manufactured by the *Elers*, imitated by their successors, and perfected by *Wedgwood* in his black basalt. Of this we have not seen any authentic specimens, but in the aforesaid museum are two teapots of a dead black clay, stamped with seals, and showing the characteristic hawthorn flowers, or vine leaves. They were presented by Enoch Wood, who knew them to be the work of *Twyford* (one of their imitators), as the label attached to the pieces and written by his own hand testifies. Genuine pieces of *Elers* ware are now exceedingly scarce; but imitations are very numerous, and these are constantly mistaken for real specimens. They continued to be made long after the brothers had left the country. Thus, Shaw mentions the indenture, date 1750, of one J. Fletcher, who was apprenticed to *J. Taylor*, "to handle and stick legs to the red porcelain." The identification becomes sometimes difficult when we have to deal with some of these jugs or teapots, which, bearing the same branch of Chinese blossoms, were later on manufactured in so many places; but we give the following as the results of our observations:—First, seldom, if ever, did the *Elers* produce anything of large dimensions; the most authentic pieces are of a very small size. Next, the decoration is confined principally to lines and bands sharply turned on the lathe, and accompanied with a few flowers or small scrolls stamped in relief with the seal. Lastly, in no case do they show any part that has been pressed in a mould. Spouts and handles modelled into ornamental shapes, such as are to be seen on many pieces which otherwise possess all the peculiarities of the *Elers* ware, are always a sign that these are the works of one of their successors. As to the pseudo-Chinese marks, these are to be found on the imitations as well as upon the originals, and cannot in any way be relied upon as guides to identification.

In Germany, a few years later, *Bottcher* was making what he also called Red Porcelain. The outward likeness between the two productions is probably fortuitous; at all events there can be no confusion between them, as the German red pieces are pressed, the ornaments being obtained by moulding instead of stamping. As to the name of Red Porcelain being applied to both, it should be remembered that at that time all Oriental ware, whatever its kind or colour, was called porcelain, and these varieties did not purport to be imitations of the translucent ware which we now call porcelain, but only of the fine red pottery imported from China and Japan. Furthermore, we hear of *Dwight* describing his "grès" Stone-ware as "grey porcelain," and porcelain is also the name given by *Place* to his mottled-ware.

The etymology of the word cannot be said to have been very satisfactorily traced, and numerous and far-fetched are the speculations about it. Not the least curious is that of Dr. Johnson, generally so cautious in his assertions, who gives it as coming from the French "Pour cent ans," because it was a common belief that the materials for making it had previously to be buried for a hundred years. Another strange derivation is the one from the name of King Porcena; tradition says that in his endeavours to avoid being poisoned, he discovered a kind of cup which would not hold poison without breaking. It is well known that for a long time all vessels coming from the East were popularly credited in Europe with the same astonishing property, hence the name of Porcena's ware or Porcellena! What we know is, that the word was used in a general way before being restricted to translucent ware.

Some doubts have been raised about the introduction of Salt-glaze into Staffordshire, and as to the making of the white and thin Stone-ware so peculiar to old English Pottery. Tales have been circulated which attribute to a local man the invention of glazing with salt. They say that an earthen pot filled with salt water was left on a kitchen fire, and that the brine boiled over the sides of the pot, which when cold was found to be glazed by the vapours. *Palmer*, of Bagnall, we are further told, saw it and availed himself of the discovery. It is not possible to discuss seriously the probability of such an incident having ever occurred, for the silicate can only be produced in a closed oven heated to a very high temperature, so that story has to be set aside, to take its place amongst the many fanciful tales which abound in Ceramic lore. In the dialogue given by Ward in his "*History of Stoke-upon-Trent*," we see that the question of the *Elers* having been the first to make Salt-glaze was a common topic of conversation on the ale benches. Much has been done, we are sorry to say, with a view of depriving the foreigners of what credit they were entitled to for laying down the rudiments of a new art which was to be the starting point of all the pottery manufacturers of the country. Now that we are able to look back impartially on this controversy, we can safely conclude that they were not only the creators of that special process, but also that they must at once have brought it to perfection.

In favour of the contrary opinion, Shaw ("*History of the Staffordshire Potteries*") brings forward many arguments, but they are far from conclusive. He contends that for a long time previous the Staffordshire potters ought to have been acquainted with Salt-glazing, from the knowledge they had of what Dr. Plot calls kelp, and describes as being the "'Fucus Maritimus,' which in the Isle of Thanet is burned to ashes, put into vessels, and carried over to Holland, with which they glaze all their earthenware." Here Shaw falls into a rather ludicrous mistake for a chemist. The ashes he mentions are the alkalis used in the composition of stanniferous enamel, and not at all the salt employed for the glazing of Stone-ware by evaporation. He also states that he heard from the oven builders who pulled down the last of the ovens left by the *Elers*, that it was a common biscuit oven, having nothing of the appliances necessary to fire Salt-glaze. We need hardly say that this was probably the one in which they fired their red-ware; the others, erected for different purposes, were, no doubt, demolished a long time before, becoming useless when glazing with salt was completely abandoned.

Had any systematic digging been carried out on the *Elers'* ground, the fragments discovered would at once have settled the question. Unfortunately nothing has so far been brought to light excepting a few bits of their red-ware. But an undisputed fact remains, which goes far towards proving that they glazed with salt, and that the practice was quite an unprecedented one in the country. Aitkins (*"History of Manchester"*) relates that the Burslem potters assembled, eight in number, round the *Elers'* new ovens, to protest against the volumes of smoke they emitted. What other sort of firing could have so created smoke as to frighten the natives, who by this time were certainly used to the smoke of their own ovens? Salt-glazing, which was at a later date to darken the streets of Burslem in such a way as to render them all but impassable, could alone have so taken them by surprise. Mr. Gatty quotes from *Josiah Wedgwood's* papers a note written by his own hand in 1765, containing the particulars supplied to him by a workman named Steel, aged 84, who could remember the Dutchmen at work at Bradwell, and who joined those who ran to the spot, amazed at this unusual mode of firing.

Steel also states that the Salt-glaze ware was first made by the Dutchmen. This should by itself be a sufficient proof. We may add that if Salt-glazing had been discovered and practised by *Palmer* in 1680, Dr. Plot, who wrote in 1686, and goes into such minute particulars, would not have failed to mention it.

It is to be regretted that we have so few documents to help us when we endeavour to ascertain the truth about the potters of that time, but a deep mystery surrounded their researches and their labour. *Bottcher*, while experimenting upon his new bodies, was actually kept a prisoner in the fortress of Koenigstein, by the Elector of Saxony. The *Elers* seem to have worked in the most profound seclusion, taking every precaution to prevent anyone from prying into their secrets, and being very particular about the sort of people they employed as assistants. Only those who looked dull of understanding were admitted on to the premises; to be an idiot was a recommendation for anyone engaged to turn the wheel while the master was throwing the ware, or to manipulate the clay which had previously been mixed in secrecy. The goods when finished were brought by night from Bradwell to Dimsdale, and only at the latter place were customers allowed to enter.

As might have been expected, so many precautions were certain to excite curiosity. Idiots were not wanting when asked for. Two shrewd men took the trouble to personate the character, and through that artifice *Astbury* and *Twyford* succeeded in witnessing all the manipulations, and mastering most of the secrets. Their conduct, if the tale of the abject deception they kept up for more than two years is true, is not much to their credit, but it is fair to say that *Astbury* afterwards atoned for his duplicity, and redeemed his reputation. He did more than profit by knowledge so dishonourably acquired, for it is to him we owe the great discovery of the value of flint in the earthenware body.

In 1710 the *Elers* are said to have left Staffordshire, and one may well wonder why they ever came into such a place. Aliens among a strange people, who had perhaps never seen a foreigner in their lives, making a secret of all their doings, while everybody in the trade was working in the light of day; selling their teapots in London at a guinea a-piece, while the entire production of other potters hardly averaged four pounds a week; and, above all, retaining probably their refined and aristocratic manners amongst a people who had so far advanced but little beyond their primitive roughness; jealousy was rife around them, and life for them must have been anything but pleasant. They had indeed nothing to do but go; and away they went, leaving behind them as at once a pattern and a reproach, their works—a sure guide towards that perfection to which their successors endeavoured to attain.

John Philip Elers gave up his business in reduced circumstances, and on his arrival in London became connected with the glass manufactory established in Chelsea in 1676, by Venetians, under the auspices of the Duke of Buckingham. So says Shaw *("Chemistry of Pottery")*; no other document has ever corroborated the assertion, but in our collection is an *Elers* teapot, which is decorated all over with scrolls of white and coloured enamels similar to those which might have been used in a glass manufactory.

We have always spoken of the brothers jointly in all we have said concerning their life and their works, so adhering to tradition, though we believe John Philip alone was the potter. At the end of their career we find them separated. Again we lose sight of David, but learn from the particulars given to *Josiah Wedgwood* by Edgeworth, that John Philip went to Dublin, where, with the assistance of Lady Barrington, he set up a glass and china shop, and became very prosperous in business. (Miss Meteyard's "*Life of Wedgwood.*")

After their departure, the new ways of potting they had introduced, though kept up in the main, underwent some transformations. Making a compromise between the old style and the new, *Astbury* continued to apply ornaments on the red clay, ornaments impressed with small metal seals, but he used white clay to contrast them with the ground, and glazed them over with galena.

At Shelton, where stood his manufactory, many fragments were discovered a few years ago. They are all pieces of tea and coffee ware, made of the fine red clay, richly glazed and ornamented with white embossments; among the ornaments are the royal arms, the fleur-de-lys, and birds and flowers, somewhat different in design from the *Elers'* seals, and far from equalling in finish the perfection of the red porcelain; but neatness of execution seems to have given way to a desire for brightness of colour. Various coloured grounds are chosen to set out the relief; upon the shining black clay run white branches of vine; little yellow cocks stand out on the shining red. The red clay is applied in the shape of hawthorn blossoms upon the yellow or buff body, the most elaborate and finely stamped specimens being of a saffron yellow ground, covered with scrolls and leaves of great delicacy. Sometimes we have a would-be Chinese figure; the whole enlivened by touches of flowing and transparent colour, such as are used on the tortoiseshell-ware. The handles and knobs are in all cases of the same clay as the ornaments, and were still made by hand.

For a long time afterwards stamping was used to complete the ware turned on the wheel, whether it be white Salt-glaze, or earthenware coloured and glazed with lead. Red porcelain was still made, but how different in quality! We possess a huge red teapot profusely decorated with branches and rosettes done by the old process; it has been silver-mounted, which shows that some value was set upon it, yet it is so coarse in execution that it could not stand comparison with any of the earlier pieces. We have also an identical replica of the small red teapot, preserved at Etruria, as the first piece made by *Wedgwood* during his apprenticeship; but the raised blossoms spread upon it are made in the German way, that is to say, moulded separately and stuck on the surface, and we greatly doubt its being of English origin.

Pottery took advantage of all the great events of the time. A new sort of ware was made to spread the news of a victory, or to commemorate its glory. In 1727 *Astbury* created the Portobello ware, which had a great run after the expedition of—

> "Admiral Vernon, that brave fellow (who)
> With six ships took Porto-bello."

Dies were sunk in the shape of ships, and whole flotillas were stamped in white on the red tea-ware. In the British Museum is a very fine bowl so decorated. On other pieces the full-length figure of the hero is represented, and also a conventional view of the fortifications. Mr. H. Willet has two different Salt-glaze teapots made in honour of the admiral.

Of *Astbury* and his discoveries a good deal more will be said hereafter. We have only spoken of him here in connection with the stamped-ware, and as being the worthiest successor of the *Elers*. Trained by the foreigners, as it were, he altered and improved their fabric into one of genuine English character in all its particulars—manufacture as well as design.

CHAPTER VI.

SALT-GLAZE.

Origin of the White Stone-Ware glazed with Salt.—Salt-Glaze Ovens in Burslem.—The Glaze and its high degree of Firing. —Composition of the Body.—Stamped Ornaments and Brass Moulds.—Mould Cutting.—Casting.—Introduction of Plaster Moulds.—Extension of the Pottery Trade in Staffordshire. —Astbury and the other leading Potters of the Period. —Variety of Shapes and their Originality.—Different processes connected with the Salt-Glaze Ware.— Scratched Blue.—Competition with the German Ware.—Enamelled Salt-Glaze.—Gilding.—Reproduction of China pieces made in Salt-Glaze Ware.—Tiles.—Perforated Pieces. —Localities where Salt-Glaze was Manufactured.

SALT-GLAZE.

WHITE Earthen vessel, daintily formed, delicately embossed with graceful arabesques or flowers, and which shows under a pellucid glaze brightening but not hiding the sharpness of the most minute details, a semi-transparence in the thinnest parts of the substance. Does not the description read as if some sort of Porcelain was intended? and yet we only applied it in our own mind to English Salt-glaze, the new ware which was once opposed in England to the heavily-made and darkly-coloured earthenware, the brown stone or the clumsy Delft, the only fictile productions of the period. With this discovery the potters thought for a time that they could compete with importations from the East; at least that they were on the verge of solving the mystery of the Chinese porcelain, the wonder of all European countries, a mystery so difficult to penetrate that for some time it was coupled with the secret of the philosopher's stone. Distant as it was from a perfect imitation, yet its success was immense, and its use suddenly spread all over the kingdom.

In the chapter on Stone-ware, a ware also glazed with salt, we have described the chemical action of the silica of the paste upon the vapours of the soda contained in the common salt, and how by this means the glaze is formed upon the ware. We have also said that any clay refractory enough to stand a sufficiently high temperature can from ordinary earthenware be transformed into stone-ware, that is to say, may show a commencement of vitrification all through the texture of the body; a still higher degree of heat could even fuse it into a glass; but in this case the fusion is uncontrollable, and no transparent ware could safely be made out of it. This was one of *Dwight's* difficulties in his searches after Porcelain. Even in the Potteries, when the composition of the paste had been settled after protracted experiments, too much fire caused the ware to melt. We have seen many examples of cast-away saggers with all the pieces they contained sticking to each other and sunk at the bottom in a shapeless mass.

The glaze offers this peculiarity, that it does not run and spread like other glazes, but remains in the state of minute drops or granulations; its surface can be compared to leather or orange peel. These particles are more or less conspicuous according to the conditions of the firing. Sometimes when red lead was added to the salt the fluidity of the mixture makes them hardly perceptible. Often the gloss is unequally distributed over the pieces; although the saggers in which they were enclosed for protection were pierced with large holes, the vapours of soda did not reach every place in the same proportion, so occasionally one side may be quite dry while the other is highly glazed.

At an early date white-ware glazed with salt was made in Germany, and thence carried to England. We cannot doubt that *Dwight* made at Fulham a kind of white Stone-ware glazed with salt, but the lack of any authenticated specimens leaves us in the dark as to its exact properties. Such as it stands now preserved in many diversified examples in the cabinets of the collectors, the thin "Salt-glaze," as we shall henceforth call the English white Stone-ware, was, we believe, created in the district where it was so extensively manufactured, viz., the Staffordshire Potteries.

We have already stated upon what grounds the introduction of the process may be attributed to *John Philip Elers;* at all events it was only a few years after he had settled down at Bradwell, and astonished the inhabitants with his unwonted way of firing, that Salt-glaze ovens were erected all over the town of Burslem. It is reported that so many factories were at work at that time, that on Saturday mornings, when the fires were at their highest and drawing towards the end, the smoke emitted was so dense that the passer-by had to grope his way, as in the midst of the thickest London fog, amongst fumes "not unlike the smoke of Mount Vesuvius." On the scaffolds that surrounded the oven, several men stood opposite the apertures of each of the flues, shovelling the salt into the fire, and every time they fed the fiery mouths the flames, driving away for a moment the murky smoke, revealed to view the men wrapped in clothes soaked with water, and their faces protected with wet sheets.

No marks, no dates, come to elucidate the problem of when and by whom the first pieces were made. Here again we are reduced to speculation. Contradictory statements are in existence; we can dismiss some of them on account of their improbability, acknowledging at the same time that something might be learnt from them if we could only understand their real purport, instead of continuing to be misled by the inappropriate terms in which they are worded.

When the attention of collectors was first drawn to these curious and undescribed pieces, they were erroneously called "Elizabethan Ware." We have now made it clear that the mistake arose out of a jug of that manufacture being preserved in Shakespear's House, at Stratford, and having been known for a long time by the name of "Shakespear's Jug."

We cannot, knowing the conditions of temperature required for Salt-glazing, place any reliance upon the tradition which attributes its discovery to *Palmer*, of Bagnall, in 1680. The tale, as reported by several authors, says that a servant had left on the fire a pot full of salt-water, and the brine overboiling, covered the outside of the pot with a bright glaze; a surprising fact which the potter immediately turned to account, and put into practice in his factory. It is an utter impossibility, and therefore this long-credited story may be regarded as disposed of.

If it is not true that the *Elers* introduced Salt-glazing into Staffordshire, we at all events have proof that this manufacture did not prevail in the Potteries very early in the 18th century. From the perusal of the list of the Burslem potters between 1710 and 1715, we see there were only six ovens in that town turning out Stone-ware, and even then no special mention is made of its being glazed with salt; not one potter was making it in Hanley.

It is probable that about that time the Staffordshire potters, by mixing the whitish clay found at Shelton with the fine sand of Baddeley Edge, or else the cane marl with the grit from Mow Cop, began to make a fire-resisting body which could stand the required temperature. To these materials was also added, before the discovery of flint, the white clay employed by the pipemakers, and with which were made the first experiments for a white ware. Pipes had been manufactured at Newcastle-under-Lyme, as well as in many other places, years before Dr. Plot visited the Potteries; he describes how *Charles Riggs*, of Newcastle, made them of three different sorts of clays, the best of which was found between Shelton and Hanley Green. Many of these pipes, impressed with the initials of the maker, have been from time to time dug out in quantities; and as they are quite white and well fired, surprise might be felt that the same material had not been turned into good account for the making of pots. The reason is that the lead ore then used for glazing did not allow of any white ware being made, as it turned the whitest biscuit to a dingy yellow tint, but as soon as the colourless glaze obtained with salt was discovered, pipe-clay became the basis of many new compounds.

In the Potteries, no materials were employed at first but those procured on the spot; with the marl, the clays from the coal measures, and the sand also found in the locality, they made the "buff" ware; for white ware they had the pipe-clay and the grit excavated from the Mow Cop strata; the requisite salt was obtained from the neighbouring mines of Cheshire; thus it could fairly be called a genuine Staffordshire ware. We shall hereafter show how its shapes and decorations may also set up an unquestionable claim to originality.

We feel inclined to suppose that a "buff" body was first attempted with the same clay as that used for common stone pots, and that the white pipe-clay was then confined to such small raised ornaments as were sparingly applied on the surface; the ware did not become quite white until it had passed through many successive improvements all aiming in that direction. The earliest kind was of a greenish tint, and was called "Crouch-ware." That term, which has puzzled more than one, comes from the name of the white Derbyshire clay; long before being used for Salt-glaze it had been employed at

Nottingham to make crucibles and glass pots, and under the name of "Crouch clay" it figures in several old documents.

Most of the early pieces bear such a striking resemblance to the red porcelain of the *Elers*, in potting as well as in ornamentation, that it is difficult not to ascribe the same origin to both wares.

The Crouch-ware is of a dense paste; if not quite so hard as the red porcelain, it is because the ferric oxide contained in the latter increases its vitreousness. The shapes, neatly formed, are equally well finished on the lathe; and a pressed part is never added to them, excepting perhaps occasional feet or claws supporting some of the teapots, impressed in the "pitcher" mould of one single piece called a "thumb mould."

In his MS. notes, *Josiah Wedgwood* relates that the *Elers* introduced moulds of plaster of Paris; we cannot trust this assertion, as it is not corroborated by any known example; on the contrary, from all that has come under our notice, and other collateral proofs, we can deduce the fact that they did not employ any moulds, either of plaster or terra cotta; they stamped on and did not press separately the applied ornaments, differing in this particular from *Dwight*, who worked by the latter process. We find in his notes mention of a "grey clay to be 'spriged' with white;" the term is still used in our days, and means to stick on the surface the relief taken out of a mould. We shall insist upon the point that in the *Elers*' ware all the ornaments are stamped on the piece itself with small metal seals, as can be ascertained by the impression of the die, the square ground of which is seen sunk in the clay round the raised subjects. Made in this way, we have many remarkable pieces of buff colour, relieved by rosettes and entwined lines of white clay, not unlike in design the typographic ornaments of the period; the forms are finely turned and finished, and seldom show any defect, but the applied parts have cracked in many places, as though the difficulty of making the two clays agree together had not yet been completely mastered. Enoch Wood's collection was especially rich in specimens of this ware, now so difficult to obtain, and that fact tends to prove that it was made in the Potteries. Pieces of the same description are also found having a wash of white clay in the inside, or even made entirely of the white body; these may safely be attributed to the successors of

13

the *Elers*, who continued to work in their style long after the Dutchmen had left the country.

As the new ware was especially admired on account of its thinness and delicacy, all efforts were made to insure these qualities; spoons, sauce boats, and small trays were manufactured as light as wafers, by means of copper or lead moulds, which acted like our goffering irons, impressing them at one blow on the outer and inner surfaces. The notion of such moulds was no doubt derived from the usual brass seals; they have now become very scarce, yet some of them are preserved in the Geological Museum and in the Hanley Institute.

Pieces of larger dimensions were cast in "pitcher" or terra-cotta moulds. Here we shall describe the peculiar process by which models and moulds were made; instead of modelling the form in relief as we should now-a-days, it was hollowed out of several pieces of native gypsum, which formed the different sections of the intended mould; after they had been graven and sunk with complicated patterns of flowers and scrolls, a proof was taken, and, being fired in the oven, it became what was called the "block;" upon this block an unlimited number of clay moulds could be made, all of which preserved the sharpness of the original work.

By examining the style of embossments of the Salt-glaze ware, we perceive at once how well the decoration is contrived to allow of its being conveniently carved in the hollow shell of the mould; each section has a separate subject, and the seams existing between the sections, which are the great trouble of the potter who would try to conceal them, have been made use of in the composition as partition lines which divide it into panels. The subjects were always selected with the view of affording the greatest facility of execution. For instance, the "mould cutters," as they were called, found the "pecten" shell, with its many ribs, especially appropriate to their style of carving, so they brought it to bear in an endless variety of combinations, and with it are associated such small foliage and lines as can be conveniently engraved in the mould with a single stroke of the gouge. It has been advanced that the earliest models were taken from silver plate pieces. The fact is patent with respect to some of the china made at Bow, Chelsea, and Worcester, but does not apply to Salt-glaze ware. This had a style of its own, which in no way recalls the "repoussé" or chased work of the silversmiths.

In the "pitcher" moulds the ware was not pressed, but cast; the process of casting consisted in filling the mould with diluted clay or slip, then pouring it out, leaving a thin coat of clay on the surface; as soon as it began to dry the operation was repeated, and each time the coating increased in thickness. When the required strength had been obtained the whole was placed before the fire, and by desiccation the mould separated from the piece; it was then ready to be garnished with the handles, spouts, or claws, which had been separately cast in the same way. The pieces made in "terra cotta" or brass moulds are the most ancient, and are far superior in sharpness of detail and style of execution to the comparatively modern ones cast in plaster moulds. These latter were easily deteriorated, and as they were still used after having been quite worn out, very poor stuff was produced as soon as they superseded the "pitcher" moulds. It was not until 1750 that *Ralph Daniel,* of Burslem, brought back from a porcelain manufactory in France the first mould in plaster of Paris; the innovation was adopted at once by the other potters of the town, and it afforded great facilities for quickness of production, but often at the expense of neatness and quality. At the same date "pressing," that is to say, moulding with a thick lump of clay, began to be substituted for casting, and the daintily embossed pieces soon disappeared altogether.

But to return to the introduction of Salt-glaze into the Potteries, and the influence it had upon the general trade of the country, we must once more call to mind the fact that pottery in that district had so far been only a modest craft, by which the master could in his single thatched hovel average only a produce of the value of four or five pounds a week, out of which all expenses had to be paid. About eight men were employed at each place; and the best workman who could throw, turn, and handle, had to divide his time, and work for two or three factories in the same week.

The introduction of the new white ware was to turn this small trade into a large industry. The one oven of each potter had to be increased in size to answer the demand, and soon, to the astonishment of the inhabitants of Shelton, *R. & J. Baddeley* erected four ovens in a row behind their manufactory. Instead of being limited to the consumption of the adjoining counties, the ware began to be carried away to all parts of England. Business connections were established with distant towns. Carriers were sent off with a load of goods, to sell them and take further orders; but the way of trading was still very primitive. "When they came home," says Shaw, "after having disposed of their stock, they simply emptied the money bag of its contents, without rendering any account of their transactions."

Notwithstanding the cheapness of labour at the time, the care bestowed upon these delicate little pieces made them rather expensive in comparison with the common earthen pots, and we think that Salt-glaze remained for a long time the highest class of ware, and was paid for accordingly. Though the size of the ovens had been enlarged, and the weekly production greatly increased, little of it was kept for home use, but the ware was sent away to be sold everywhere to well-to-do people. In my experience of old pot hunting in Staffordshire, I have hardly found any Salt-glaze pieces in the cottages; all I have gathered together, though mostly manufactured in the Potteries, came from other counties. I may, however, say that they stood more chances of being destroyed than any other ware, being so fragile, and liable to break in hot water.

Astbury and *Twyford* took the lead in the manufacture of Salt-glaze, the former employing the Bideford pipe-clay and the Devon and Dorset clays, which from the ports whence they were obtained were called Chester clays. They therefore departed from the custom of using local materials only. *Astbury* washed with these clays the inner surfaces of his buff Stone-ware, and made also a white stone body which he still further improved by making ground flint the principal ingredient of it.

Thomas Billing, in 1722, took out a patent "for making the most refined earthenware, of a nature and composition not only transparent, but so perfect in its kind as, contrary to the nature of all other earthenwares, to resist almost any degree of heat." The specification of transparency here indicates a sort of Salt-glaze, while the inventor was trying to overcome the objection put forth against its general use, by boasting, like many others, of having found the means of remedying that imperfection.

Ralph Shaw, of Burslem, took out a patent, in 1732, for a

chocolate ware, which was white inside and glazed with salt. We shall have occasion to refer to him more fully in the next chapter.

Dr. Thomas Wedgwood was the principal potter of Burslem at that time, making various kinds of ware besides Salt-glaze. To him, in 1731, was apprenticed *Aaron Wood*, who attained to the greatest reputation as "block cutter and mould maker," and enjoyed the privilege of working in a room by himself, locked up by his employer. He was to work for no one else but his present master, and the master in his turn promises that he will "employe him in, but himself only." Some of the moulds made by *A. Wood* have been preserved, and bear his name scratched in the paste; one of them is in the South Kensington Museum.

Thomas & John Wedgwood established themselves at Burslem as makers of white Stone-ware before 1740, and by experimenting on the liability to crack of various clays, introduced many improvements in its manufacture. Their enterprising spirit was generally censured, and considered little short of extravagance. They erected a spacious manufactory covered with tiles, while all the others were still covered with thatch, and they had three ovens built on their premises.

The brothers *Baddeley*, who at the same time had four ovens erected in a row behind their workshops, made elegant white Stone-ware, including fruit baskets, and bread or sweet trays, cast in moulds, and exhibiting ornaments on both sides.

Aaron Wood and *William Littler* made the first blue Salt-glaze, which was said to resemble the finest "*lapis lazuli*."

Many other names might be added to this list, but the above are sufficient to show how the potters tried to rival each other, and bring out some improvement in their specialities. Unfortunately, however varied and distinct are the specimens, very few of them can safely be attributed to any of these makers in particular, so little care has been taken to preserve the traditions by which not long ago many might have been identified.

The imagination of the Staffordshire "block cutters" was very fertile in quaint devices; for instance, in the case of simple tea-pots they seem to have exhausted every conceivable shape. We have tea-pots that are globular, elliptic, octagonal, square, and oblong; others that are formed like two or more shells; and others again that are heart-shaped, and called for this reason "lovers' tea-pots." All sorts of animals or figures are used; a squirrel, or a bird, a bear with its cub, and a Bacchus astride his cask. This last was probably made by or for *Thomas Bacchus*, a potter, who married *Astbury's* widow. We know not fewer than five different shapes of camel tea-pots, and still more in the shape of a house, nearly all these being represented in our collection. Sometimes the artist gives vent to his fancy, and models by hand a little group, which was not to be reproduced. Such is the interesting example in Mr. Willett's collection of a lady seated in the church pew with her two grown up sons by her side. We have also a quaint figure of a queen, probably Queen Anne, dating from the same period. Children's toys were also made, such as birds with whistles in their tails, or flowers on a stand. M. A. Franks has an exquisite toy tea service. Purely ornamental pieces also began to be manufactured, such as spill vases, flower-pots, and hanging brackets, but in no case do they exhibit any attempt to imitate a foreign model. They are, on the contrary, striking instances of what can be done with an art which, born on the soil, there gradually develops itself without any extraneous assistance.

A collection formed with the view to illustrate all the different kinds of Salt-glaze ware, would in itself comprise innumerable varieties of pieces and processes, so diversified were the transformations the fabric was made to undergo; from the massive jar, impervious and indestructible, the material of which could not be surpassed for the uses to which it was put, to dainty little cups, the prettiness of which rivals porcelain. Long before salt-glazing had made its appearance in England, "Grès" Stone-ware had been manufactured in Germany, and brought to a high degree of excellence. There the theme had its origin, but the English potter added to it endless variations. He was the first who attempted to impart to his Stone-ware a lightness of substance and a gloss of surface which could render it fit for all sorts of decorations. Setting aside the brown pieces made in imitation of German ones, of which we have spoken in a previous chapter, we shall try to briefly describe the varieties which would constitute a complete collection of Salt-glaze. These are:—

Ornaments of white clay, stamped with seals, on a buff or white body, in the style of the *Elers*.

Flowers or foliage "sprigged" on to the piece, that is to say, made in a separate mould and stuck on with slip, the stems which join them together being made by hand with a strip of clay.

Thin pieces covered with embossments made in copper or "pitcher" moulds, in all sorts of picturesque forms, body of greyish or dull yellow colour, glaze dry.

Engine-turned pieces in great variety.

Mixtures of coloured bodies in the style of the Agate-ware.

Combinations of the common red clay with a coating of white Stone-ware, the scratching of the upper coat showing the dark clay underneath in the same way as the Italian *Sgrafiato*.

Pieces made in plaster moulds, white body, thicker in substance and less sharp in execution.

Perforated dishes and basket ware.

Pressed tiles, with landscapes in relief.

The processes for surface decoration are also very numerous.

Some of the early embossed pieces are spotted with patches of cobalt blue. Upon others the ornaments are scratched with a point and the lines filled in with powdered zaffre.

Light blue Stone-ware paste used for applied ornament or for the ground in the same manner as blue jasper.

Decoration with dots of red slip or lines of manganese.

Deep cuttings in the body with a blade, diamond shape, or diagonal lines as upon some German pieces.

Shavings of clay strewn on the surface so as to form rough bands alternating with smooth ones, or all over the pieces as in the bears.

Blue Salt-glaze, the whole piece covered with a blue ground under the glaze.

Tin-glaze combined with the Salt-glaze, either for the ground or painted on in opaque decoration.

Enamelling in all sorts of styles.

Size gilding or varnish painting.

Printing in red or black, etc.

Some of the above processes deserve special attention. The "scratched blue" for instance enjoyed a successful run. The ware is as neatly potted as it is barbarously decorated. After having been turned it passed into the hands of women called "flowerers," who with a point scratched in the wet clay a cursive pattern, and with a flock of cotton wool dusted powdered zaffre in the hollow lines. They never attained to a very high proficiency, nor does any potter seem to have ever taken care to supply them with good patterns. Jugs and mugs of this ware were in great demand for public houses, and unlike other specimens of Salt-glaze, they often bear dates and inscriptions, many of them referring to elections and other public events. The gift of a mug was one form of bribery. One of them, preserved in the British Museum, has: "Sir William a plumper." Another, in Lady Charlotte Schreiber's collection, is inscribed with four verses in honour of the King of Prussia, 1758. In our own collection a circular pocket flask is dated 1766. All the pieces that have come under our notice relate to the same period.

Earlier than these, and still more clumsy in decoration, are the jugs and mugs, made evidently in competition with the German "Grès" Stone-ware, which have a medallion, or simply the crowned monograms of George I. and George II. They are ribbed on the top and bottom, and all round heavy leaves are incised and stained over with a rag dipped in liquid blue. These are sometimes attributed to Fulham, but fragments have often been found in the Potteries, a fact which tends to prove that these jugs were made there.

About 1750, Salt-glaze, which so far had been decorated with only random touches of blue or brown, was thought fit to receive enamel decoration, with the intention of thereby rivalling the costly china made at Chelsea and Worcester. As the manufacturers of these last-named places chiefly aimed at reproducing the patterns of Eastern Porcelain, so did the first enamellers in Staffordshire, and it is not to be wondered at if painting on Salt-glaze did not keep in the track of originality opened by the first "block cutters." Besides, the earliest pieces were not, and could not be, painted by local artists, as no hands had yet been trained to that style of decoration. Two painters came from Holland and settled in Hot Lane, near Burslem. They used to buy white Stone-ware from the potters and enamel it in great secrecy, painting it with flowers and figures in a pseudo-Chinese manner. For a long time the manufacturers were dependent on decorators wholly unconnected with their pot works. Private persons came from Liverpool, Bristol, and Worcester, for the purpose of buying

Salt-glaze ware to decorate it on the spot. This practice was all the easier as only a small muffle was required for enamel painting.

Very soon the number of artists so employed in the Potteries became considerable, but improvements were not quickly effected in a locality so remote as the Potteries was at that time. The potters could not seek any help or derive any hints from any other collateral branch of the trade. In large towns, where stained glass windows were painted, and where goldsmiths covered their work with bright enamels, they might have been earlier made acquainted with recipes of colours and enamels which would have met their special wants. It was indeed in this way that the first china painters proceeded on the Continent, but such assistance was not available in Staffordshire, so the potters had to wait once more until foreign assistance came to the rescue.

Daniel, of Cobridge, was the first local potter who practised enamelling in his factory, and his example was soon followed by others. This was the highest improvement that could be applied to the ware. It perfected and completed its manufacture. It achieved at once a great success, principally because it became in that way a fairly good substitute for the painted china so much in fashion, but which, on account of its exorbitant price, was only to be indulged in by the wealthiest class. Either the embossments were followed by the painter, and relieved with colours, or patterns were traced across them in a free and off-hand manner. Chinese decorations were often imitated; sometimes engravings were copied, or the artist let his imagination run freely upon figure subjects, in costumes of the period. We possess a tea canister painted with garden scenes, each comprising several personages and an elaborate landscape; in front is a delicately worked ornament, something like a book plate, surrounding the words "Fine Bohea Tea;" the whole is beautifully executed. A coffee pot, also in our own collection, is painted with flowers in the Chelsea style, probably by some one who had come over from that manufactory. Many are the pieces which have the portrait of the King of Prussia, the favourite hero of the time. On a curious crabstock handle teapot, of which many copies are still in existence, his profile is enamelled in proper colour, while the whole ground is dotted over with small black strokes to represent ermine. We have several specimens of various coloured grounds—red, maroon, blue, and green; small white medallions are reserved, upon which are painted landscapes or bouquets of flowers, somewhat in the Worcester style. By the additional process of size gilding, these pieces are made to look very handsome, and there is little excuse left for their aristocratic models to give themselves airs of superiority. The enamels on all these pieces shine with the brightest hues; the turquoise blue especially would bear comparison with the best soft china colour, and they stand out all the better by the contrast they offer to the dull grey tint of the body. In many cases so much skill and finish have been bestowed on the painting, that we cannot help thinking it would attract much greater admiration if it had only been executed upon a finer material. At any rate the decoration seldom lacks the style and character so often missing from costly examples of English china. For this reason the artist cannot but look with partiality upon the best pieces of enamelled Salt-glaze, and praise their decorative effect.

The traces of half-obliterated gilding remaining on some pieces show that gold was often introduced in the decoration, but the potters did not yet know how to burn it in. We learn from *Wedgwood's* letters that in 1765 he himself was still busy trying to overcome the difficulty. Leaf gold, secured with size or varnish, was employed, and burnishing was not practised in the Potteries until some years later, when some workmen brought the process over from the Derby manufactory.

We have said that the use of plaster moulds took away many of the artistic features of the early Salt-glaze. The facility with which casts of metal or china pieces could be taken, led to the reproduction of many admired models, and the ware, which had kept its originality for such a long time, was debased into mere copies. So we find the "bee jug," of Bow, made of white Stone-ware, and salt cellars with shells and sea-weeds, similar to those of Plymouth. In Mr. Willett's collection is a group of several figures, imitating white porcelain so perfectly that it might deceive any one at a first glance. *Wedgwood's* jasper was also imitated. Dr. Walker, of Liverpool, has two medallions on a blue ground, with applied portraits of *Josiah Wedgwood* and his wife, after the picture by Stubbs. These medallions at one time were very commonly found in the Potteries. As

Delft tiles made at Liverpool or abroad were extensively used for fire-places or decorative purposes, tiles in stamped Salt-glaze were manufactured to compete with them. We possess a set of these which came from *Whieldon's* own house. They were probably made by him, as the same patterns are also found decorated with his usual "tortoiseshell" process. They represent landscapes and animals, and the moulds used were carved after the old fashion.

The perforated china plates and dishes brought over from Dresden gave rise to a new style of dessert services, perforated on the rim, and embossed all over with basket work and various ornaments. They were not copies, but distant imitations; and a certain pattern cut in the mould by *Aaron Wood* is now in every collection. An enormous quantity must have been produced, for even in our days it would not be difficult to bring together entire services of it. In the same manner open-work fruit baskets of a fragile character, cruet stands, and puzzle jugs were made. We have a charming sweet box, formed of a double shell; the outer one, thin as an ordinary sheet of cardboard, is perforated with numerous holes which show the inner box in the same way as certain Chinese puzzles.

The manufacture of Salt-glaze was not confined to Staffordshire. At Jackfield it was made early in the 18th century, although, probably, only in imitation of the ware made in the adjoining county, and towards 1763, *Simpson* manufactured pipe-clay ware glazed with salt for the American market.

At Leeds, white and enamelled Salt-glaze preceded the manufacture of cream-coloured earthenware.

At Liverpool, quantities of "wasters" have been found on the site of *Shaw's* manufactory, and many stamped pieces bear the liver, the bird which is the crest of the town. The rare printed plates may also have been made there.

At Swansea, according to Chaffers, a very thin Salt-glaze ware, roughly but effectively decorated with bright enamels, was made about 1780, and some of the specimens are marked "Cambrian Pottery." It was probably made at many other places, of which no records remain.

In our time the wafer-like white stone-ware glazed with salt has gone the way of the heavy Delft; they both had their day, and then ceased to be. A small manufactory of the former lingered at Burslem until 1823.

More, perhaps, than any other English ware, the Salt-glaze excites the interest we feel for any artistic production which speaks to us of bygone times, obsolete taste, and vanished customs; in short, it does look *old;* older, indeed, than many pieces that can boast of a much more ancient pedigree. Independently of their proper merits, an old painting darkened and mellowed by years, an oxidized bronze, a weather-beaten building, or a time-worn statue, possesses an attractive charm that age alone has imparted. A feeling of the same sort, a mingled sensation of liking and curiosity, first attracted us towards the strange-looking specimens of early Salt-glaze ware. Their soft creamy tint recalls that of old ivory, and the glossy surfaces of both offer resemblances; the designs, simple and "naif" as they are, may be compared for their conventionality to those which adorn the pages of Gothic MSS. If we add to this, that most of these embossed and wafer-like pieces have come out from the firing twisted and crooked, and so are very different from anything else the eye generally rests upon, we shall see at once how difficult it would be by a mere process of comparison with other artistic objects to ascribe any definite age to them. One can easily understand how "Elizabethan ware" was thought to be at first a suitable name, when little or nothing was known of the Staffordshire Potteries and of the potters who, for more than a century, had spread their productions all over England.

Few things are left for the amateur of the future, even for him of the present day who cannot command an unlimited supply of money; all has been collected, classified, and priced, all excepting the works of the old English Potter; many are still about, to be picked up at a small price for the gratification of the few who, like ourselves, delight in studying and admiring them. It is not too late to begin to form collections, and we hope that one day we shall see these primitive productions valued and appreciated as they deserve to be.

CHAPTER VII.

EARTHENWARE.

CREAM-COLOUR, AGATE WARE, TORTOISESHELL, ETC.

ANTIQUITY OF EARTHENWARE.—ITS REVIVAL BY ENGLISH POTTERS.—IMPROVEMENTS IN EARTHENWARE FOLLOWING ON THE RESEARCHES FOR A WHITE BODY.—INCREASE IN THE TRADE OF THE POTTERIES TOWARDS THE BEGINNING OF THE 18TH CENTURY.—INTRODUCTION OF FLINT AND CREAM-COLOUR WARE.—TORTOISESHELL AND COLOURS UNDER GLAZE.—PATENTS.—AGATE WARE.—THOMAS ASTBURY.—RALPH SHAW.—JOHN MITCHELL.—THOMAS AND JOHN WEDGWOOD.—THOMAS WHIELDON.—SHAPES AND MODELS.—IMITATIONS AND PIRACIES.—INTRODUCTION INTO THE POTTERIES OF BLUE PAINTING ON EARTHENWARE.—ENAMELLING.—FOREIGN CHINA PAINTERS WORKING IN ENGLAND.—PLASTER MOULDS AND THEIR EFFECT.—LAST IMPROVEMENTS IN CREAM-COLOUR.

EARTHENWARE.

THE history of the best English earthenware glazed with lead is so intimately linked with the records of the common pieces of the earliest time, the one being so necessarily the outgrowth of the other, that it is difficult to fix the date when the fabric entered on the course of improvements by which it gradually came to assert itself as the cheapest, the neatest, and the most suitable ware that could be contrived to supply our ordinary wants, until it superseded all the more complicated processes which previously had had their turn of fashion and success. A little more care in the potting and in the way of applying the glaze, and the vessels of the middle ages might have rivalled most of the cream-colour pieces made in the 18th century. The common marl of the country, mixed with pipe-clay and a little sand, constituted a plastic body which could be worked easily and quickly, and also fired safely; as to glazing, the lead ore or "galena" demanded but little preparation, and the colours were all obtained with the oxides of such well-known metals as were in after times thought sufficient for the production of a much higher class of ware; so the groundwork the potter had to improve upon was simple and sound. With these commonplace materials, marvels of the fictile art had occasionally been accomplished, for they were as remarkable for the beauty and purity of their shapes as the harmony of their colours. Nevertheless, earthenware potting remained stationary for a long time, as we have seen, and there was no demand for it. The lower classes were satisfied with the wooden utensils or coarse clay pans that answered their daily requirements; and for show, even well-to-do people preferred to anything else the tin dishes that most resembled the silver plate which adorned the dresser of the titled and the wealthy. On the Continent the first trials for a refined earthenware were master strokes, and should have led to an important manufacture, yet these attempts do not seem to have been followed up. What could excel, for instance, the style and cleverness of workmanship of the faïence d'Oiron, precious gems formed of the commonest clay? But nothing came of it; it was only made to gratify the fancy of a highly-gifted noblewoman, endowed with a keen sense of beauty and a craving for perfection. As soon as the inspiring spirit ceased to direct the efforts of her assistants, their art declined and passed away altogether. In Bauvaisie, at about the same period, the country people were for a time not short of ornamental and artistic pottery; the earthenware potters of Lachapelle des Pots were modelling all sorts of quaint pieces, curiously contrived in shape, and elaborately embossed; but their work differed completely from the ware made at Oiron. This latter owes its chief beauty to grace of form, and to an arrangement by which the cream-colour ground is minutely damascened with coloured clays. In the case of the ware of Lachapelle des Pots, on the other hand, the ground is all covered with rich glazes, exhausting the gamut of powerful harmonies that can be obtained with metallic oxides. The unknown potters of Bauvaisie were the forerunners of *Palissy*, who shortly afterwards showed what could be still achieved by means of the ordinary clay stained with coloured glazes; his indomitable energy and his refined taste raised his art to so high a level, that it became a hopeless task for his successors to attempt to maintain the heavy inheritance which *Palissy* bequeathed to them. The advent of the opaque glaze faïence, which had the advantage of being white and showing brighter colours, threw the works of all these great potters into the shade; their teachings were forgotten, and earthenware ran once more the risk of being relegated to the limbo of materials unworthy of receiving any artistic treatment.

Upon the old English potters devolved the honour of reviving the obsolete manufacture, and thus they became unconsciously the true successors of *Helene of Hangest* and *Palissy;* but where the great artists had only found scope for displaying their unapproachable individuality, the plodding, ingenious, and practical potters of England, working as a body, succeeded in creating, by gradual transformations, a ware so superior to all others that the potting trade of all the world benefited by their exertions.

Along with the red or brown clay the greyish marl was, as of yore, used in its native state. Both were glazed with "galena" or lead ore, by the primitive process of dusting it over the pieces through a bag of coarse cloth. Light-coloured ware was then largely made concurrently with all other kinds, but no preference seems to have been given to it, at first, over the dark red or black vessels that were commonly used; and yet its dull yellowish tint was capable of being vividly coloured, and was better intended to show the modelling of the surface. Little heed was taken of those qualities. It was chiefly employed as a coating for darker clays, for slip painting, or for applied ornamentation; few, if any, pieces were made of plain yellow clay, unless something exceptional was intended; and there was nothing to indicate the important part it was destined to play in the ceramics of the future. When researches for a white ware, glazed with salt, were being actively prosecuted in the pot works of Staffordshire, many combinations of clays had to be experimented upon, and the common earthenware was materially advanced by the experience acquired through the trials made with a view to obtain quite a different body. The production of white Stone-ware required a good deal more care and delicacy than had hitherto been bestowed upon ordinary potting, and yellow clay glazed with lead followed in the track of the newly-invented and more refined ware. Both being manufactured at the same place and by the same men, they kept abreast in the course of successive improvements; the same mould was used whether the piece was to be made of white Stone-ware and fired at a high temperature in the Salt-glaze oven, or of common clay to be coloured, glazed with lead, and submitted to a lower degree of heat; in one case to commend itself by the neatness of shape and details, in the other made attractive by its deep harmony of colours profusely flowing over the surface. It is the old contention of drawing and colour striving for precedence. We may be allowed to remark here that richness of hue seems to have been the natural bent of English taste. In its early and most genuine productions it affects a decided tendency towards bright and showy colours. It is only when the fact is denounced by some cold-blooded reformer that people seem to rush unanimously to the opposite extreme, discarding what they best liked. Ashamed one day of their natural feelings of admiration, they allow themselves to be talked into accepting anything that may be palmed off upon them as models, and so the conventionality and stiffness of a so-called high style may be substituted for the charms of a genuine and unsophisticated art. In Pottery as in painting, the English artist begins by showing himself a true colourist, and yet the lively and harmonious earthenware of the outset had to make room for the dull and formal cream colour and monochrome ware of the end of the 18th century. We may well ask what had become of the promise contained in the powerful productions of the tortoiseshell period; misplaced self-criticism and a too severe repression of innate propensities more than once waylaid English art and turned it from its natural channel.

During the whole course of the 17th century, many different processes were in embryo amongst the potters of Staffordshire, but production was limited, and little progress was being made, when suddenly a rage for improvement sets in, and within a few years pervades the whole district. Everyone is at work bringing his small stone to the monument. Some are sedulously engaged mixing and trying all clays and minerals that can be procured at home; others, more enterprising, take the unwonted step of travelling long distances in quest of fresh materials and suggestive models. With an astounding rapidity changes follow upon changes, pottery is applied to all sorts of fresh uses, ovens are built all over the district, and a flourishing trade is established for exportation as well as home consumption. Notwithstanding the rapid increase of population in the surrounding country, farmers find themselves short of hands; crops can hardly be gathered in, and tradesmen in towns cannot any longer obtain apprentices. All men and women go to the pot works, where there is never a sufficient supply of labour, and where wages soon grow to be uncommonly high for skilful workmen.

The numerous patents granted at that time in connection with earthenware are a sign of the prevalent excitement and the general desire for novelties. We shall give further on a few of their specifications, though little can be made of their obscure phraseology. They have only a secondary interest for us, when we remember that important discoveries which caused a revolution in the trade were never patented at all. The most interesting and effectual innovations bore upon the two principal desiderata of the potters of the day; namely, obtaining a perfectly white body, which, being easily formed into shape, should not crack in the firing, and a colourless fluid glaze. Up to that time, as we have seen, the lightest ware was of a dull, smoky tint, still darkened by the thick coating of sulphuret of lead, either dusted over the piece or unevenly applied with a hair pencil. These two wants were supplied by *Astbury's* introduction of flint bodies, and at an interval of thirty years, by *E. Booth's* method of dipping the ware into an improved glaze kept in suspension in water.

As soon as *Astbury* had fixed the exact proportion of flint that was to enter into its composition, the earthenware body may be said to have been invented and settled. We shall not question the veracity of the oft-told tale, relating how he was delayed in one of his journeys to London, to have the injured eye of his horse attended to by a farrier, who, taking a black flint stone, calcined it in the fire, then crushing it into a fine powder, blew the dust into the horse's eye; how the potter was struck with the whiteness of the material, and caused a wagon load of flint stones to be brought to Shelton, where he successfully combined the calcined powder with his ordinary clays.

The story which, by-the-by, is by some attributed to a Mr. Heath, of Shelton, may be true, or may rank amongst other doubtful anecdotes. Notwithstanding the knowledge we possess of pounded flint having been employed by *Dwight* in the composition of some of his bodies, and the probability that *Dwight* was not the first to use it, since he does not set up any claims to the discovery, it remains an undisputed fact that to *Astbury* alone was due the credit, if not of having found out quite a new material, at all events of having determined in what proportions it was to be added to the compound body which no one had made before him, and which remained for ever after, in spite of small modifications, about the same as he had left it, under whatever name his "cream colour" may have been subsequently disguised.

At first the attention of inventors was chiefly directed towards perfecting clays and glazes, and improving their manipulation; all had to be found out, and before they thought of endowing the ware with artistic qualities, they strove to secure a safe ground to work upon; this is the reason why we may now admire unreservedly their most unpretentious early pieces, the fruit of these first experiments and researches, observing how the clays are well ground and levigated; what perfection is at once reached in the turning and moulding of a simple teapot; how the lid fits well each piece; how sharp are the lines and true the shape. A good make is the main consideration, and even for decoration design comes only second to the process employed.

The most strenuous efforts of the Staffordshire potters were directed, as we have already said, towards the production of a white ware, for which there was a great demand; the flint bodies, either cream-colour glazed with lead or Salt-glazed stoneware, steadily acquired more whiteness by successive improvements; but at the same time the potters made a labour of love of experimenting upon their coloured clays and glazes, the continuation of the works of their fathers, an inheritance they jealously kept and enlarged day by day. There was no sign of their giving up making the dry red-ware, finely stamped with seals, or the highly glazed pieces of dark yellow or bright red clay relieved with coloured applications. Many continued to show their partiality for the shining black tea-ware, which made such a contrast with the spotless table-cloth, while others preferred the fanciful and ever-varied pieces brilliant with the harmonious hues of various coloured glazes.

Under the name of "clouded" or "mottled," earthenware, coloured with metallic oxides, had been for a long time before produced; this doubtless led to the imitation of tortoiseshell, so effectively carried out by means of manganese spotted with a sponge over the dry clay; simple as this process was, the aptitude of certain workmen realised with it some astonishing results, obtained by the well-contrasted shades of the opaque and the transparent parts. The success was immense, and the ware was so extensively made that the name of "tortoiseshell" extended to everything that was mottled under glaze with varied colours; we shall also keep to the same word with regard to pieces of this class whenever we may have to refer to them. Copper green, antimony, ochre yellow, manganese, and sometimes a touch of zaffre, were the only oxides used, and the colours blended in a remarkable manner, underneath a thick and smooth glaze; this was partly owing to their being fired in the same oven alternately with Salt-glaze, the brickwork and saggers being so much soaked with melted salt, that the vapours of soda pervaded all the atmosphere during the firing, acting upon the colours as a flowing agent. This method may probably account for Shaw having mistaken the old cream-colour for white stone-ware, and for his speaking of it as having been indiscriminately glazed with salt or with lead ore.

In 1724, *Robert Redrich* and *Thomas Jones* took out a patent for "staining, veining, spotting, clouding, damascening, or otherwise imitating the various kinds of marble, porphyry, and other rich stones, tortoise-shell, etc., on wood, stone, or earthenware." As they also say that the process could be applied to wood or stone, it was necessarily a surface one, and may be regarded as a derivation from that used for marbling papers; as to its application to pottery it offered little novelty, for the imitation of tortoiseshell and the combed ware had been known a long time before.

But this leads us to speak of the "*Agate-ware*" which *Dr. Thomas Wedgwood*, son of *Thomas Wedgwood*, of the Overhouse Works, at Burslem, is said to have made in great perfection; on the site of his manufactory, when digging the foundations of the new market, many fragments were disinterred. Agate-ware was a complicated process; the marbling, instead of being produced on the surface, went through the body. It was thus practised:—Thin laminæ of yellow and red clay were laid alternately upon each other until they formed a thick mass; from that mass thin slices were transversely cut with a wire, making thin bats which showed the veining produced by the superimposed layers of clays; these were then used to press the piece, the neatest side being placed against the mould. The bat required careful handling, as a pressure sideways in the wedging in or a too rough pressing in the mould destroyed the fineness in the marbling. Nothing more delicate could be formed from clay, especially when it is finished off with a clouding of bluish glaze, which makes it look like a precious stone. Only pieces of a smooth shape were made of Agate-ware, and they had to be finished on the lathe or polished by hand before firing.

Another patent was granted in 1729 to *Samuel Bell* for a new method of making a red marble Stone-ware to imitate ruby. Of this we are not able to give any account, unless it referred to a variety of bright red and yellow Agate-ware, a specimen of which is in our collection, and is the only one of the sort we ever came across.

Agate-ware, that is to say, a marbling going through the whole substance, was never made to the same extent as marbling on the surface. On the latter, *Josiah Wedgwood* made some of his favourite experiments, and he imitated very successfully and effectively all sorts of Agates and hard stones by running, mixing, and spotting various coloured slips upon the cream colour. Nearly all the potters of his day followed his lead, and produced many surface mixtures which still went by the name of Agate, although the objects on which it was used would be more properly described by the name of "marbled" ware.

Reverting to the history of the improvements brought about in the making of earthenware and cream-colour, we think we could not do better than recall the names of some of the most ingenious potters of Staffordshire, and mention the share which each had in the collective movement. Two names stand out conspicuously in the numerous list: *Astbury*, who by the introduction of flint may rightly claim to have created a new ware; and *Whieldon*, who, a few years later, brought it to so high a degree of perfection, by the care he bestowed upon its manufacture, and the taste he displayed in the selection of his models, that *Josiah Wedgwood* found little to improve in the cream-colour of his day, when he transformed it into his celebrated "Queen's ware."

Had *Astbury* ever thought, like *Palissy*, of writing his "memoirs," we should have had a book which would not have yielded in romantic interest even to the autobiography of the French potter. The business of a pot-maker was then a very precarious one. No man who was ambitious of making a fortune would have embraced that trade; the highest position a workman could hope to reach was that of owner of a single oven, turning out weekly a limited quantity of goods to be sold for a paltry profit, to the cratemen, or at the neighbouring fair. *John Astbury*, although very young, was established in a small way like his fellow-workers, and he seems to have been alive to the unsatisfactory state of the manufacture of his time; so, when the *Elers* had settled near Burslem, he could not help contrasting their delicate productions with the rough and common pottery which had up to that time been made around him. Leaving his unattractive business, he made up his mind to worm out their secrets, and thus enlarge his scanty and insufficient knowledge. What hardship he had to go through in order to get admittance into the premises without exciting suspicion has been often related. For two years, it is said, he feigned idiocy in its most abject state, until at last, considering that he had acquired all that could be mastered from his employers' processes, he threw off the disguise and set to work earnestly on his own account in quite a new style, with all sorts of fresh methods. The morals of the time admitted to a certain extent of such questionable proceedings, especially when dealing with hated foreigners. In our day such conduct would perhaps be differently regarded, and yet there is more than one redeeming point in the case of *Astbury*. We must acknowledge that he did not confine himself to reproducing exactly the same things he had seen made by the *Elers*. He originated more than one style of his own by mixing up the new notions with the old ones. The red body of his masters became in his hands a red glazed ware. The expensive piece was altered into a nearly similar one, which, by its cheapness, met the wants of the million. New articles, such as tea and coffee ware, dessert plates, and similar pieces, which had been only exceptionally made before his time, were manufactured by him in large quantities. New clays and fresh materials were unceasingly experimented upon, until a new body was at last established. Thus he tried the white clay employed by the pipe-makers; but before being able to produce a good ware from it, he used it at first as a wash inside the vessels, which, though made of red clay in the bulk, were on the inside coated with a lining of light yellow. But what entitles him to the gratitude of his contemporaries and successors is the fact that he, who had taken so much pains to get at the secrets of the Dutch potters, does not appear to have made a mystery of all that it cost him so much to acquire. He worked, after all, for the public at large. Owing to his sole exertions the whole district made rapid progress, and all the craft was benefited whenever he achieved some fresh discovery. Modest and painstaking he surely was, to judge from the manner in which he conducted his pot work. It is even said that he did not like to give free play to his inventive genius for fear of upsetting the uses and customs of his fellow-potters, and thereby come to be looked upon as a revolutionary character. There is no doubt, also, about his having been an enterprising man of business. He was one of the first who travelled to increase his connection; and at a time when, on account of the bad state of the roads, travelling was attempted by but few, he began his business tours and used to periodically make a journey to London and the large towns of the Midlands.

We have seen that towards 1720 he made his name famous by the introduction of pounded flint into common earthenware; that he would not or could not keep the discovery to himself, but that it soon spread all over the Potteries, is shown by the patent *Benson* took out, in 1726, for a new method of grinding flint-stone; heretofore, iron mortars had been used, and the dust produced by the pounding was most injurious to the health of the workmen. *Benson* conceived the idea of grinding it under water. *Astbury* was not long in realising the importance of the invention, and flint was ground in that way for the first time in a mill erected at his own expense at a place called the Ivy House, near Hanley. He died at Shelton, in 1743, being then 65 years of age, at the same place where he had started as a potter in such humble circumstances, being then a rich and highly-considered man. The site of his factory, which stood near the church, was excavated a few years ago, and many fragments were found by which the identification of his productions was greatly facilitated. He left three sons; one of them, *Thomas Astbury*, commenced business at Lane Delph in 1725; he still further improved upon the new ware invented by his father, and it was he who gave it the name of "cream-colour."

Of *Twyford*, who also played the part of an idiot to penetrate into the *Elers*' works, little is known; by some he is said to have worked conjointly with *Astbury*, by others to have had a factory of his own in the same town.

Of *Dr. Thomas Wedgwood*, and of his making a much improved ware as early as 1731, we have already spoken; he was considered the best potter of the district.

Ralph Shaw, of Burslem, had his short days of celebrity; in 1733 he patented a so-called invention for making a chocolate ware coated with white, the upper coat being scratched in with lines and flowers. One of these pieces, now become very rare, may be seen amongst the interesting specimens given by Mr. Kidd, of Nottingham, to the museum of that town. The specification of his patent was so worded that *Shaw* thought for a time it would give him the right of prosecuting most of the potters of the district for infringements. The case created great excitement when it came on for trial at Stafford; but he was not able to substantiate his claims to any exclusive rights, the same white wash having been used long before by *Astbury*, and he was non-suited. In his disappointment and humiliation he left the country, and emigrated to France with his family; there he settled and carried on his trade. It would be interesting to investigate whether it is to him that is due the first manufacture of the French "Terre de pipe," and other imitations of English ware. But to his name is attached a really valuable and practical improvement, the introduction of the "slip kiln." Previously the diluted clay had to be evaporated in the open air in large tanks called "sun pans." Not only was the evaporation slowly effected, but the slip was liable to be spoiled with dust. *Shaw* kept it under cover in long troughs, under which ran a row of flues heated from a stove outside; this expeditious process was so well appreciated that it was at once adopted at all the factories. He also found a way of firing a larger quantity of pieces in his ovens, by placing them inside each other, ingeniously parting and propping them by bits of stoneware, so that they could not stick together, an invention which led to the stilts and cockspurs of to-day. His contentious spirit may have checked for a time the course of improvements pursued by other potters, and at last it obliged him to leave a country where he might otherwise have attained to wealth and consideration. Part of his family returned to Burslem in 1750, but he himself remained abroad, and nothing is known as to the date or place of his death.

In 1736, *John Mitchell* made the same description of ware, and was one of those prosecuted by *Shaw* for infringement of his patent. Great attention was beginning to be paid at this time to the beauty of shapes and models, so *Mitchell* secured at a comparatively high price the services of *Aaron Wood*, the best block-cutter of the time, in order that he might be able to compete with *Dr. Thomas Wedgwood*, then at the head of the trade.

In 1740, *Thomas and John Wedgwood*, one a skilful fireman and the other a lead-glaze potter, established themselves at Burslem. The first few years of their partnership are said to have brought them a succession of losses and disappointments. This caused them to make a series of protracted experiments, with the especial view of ascertaining the causes of the many accidents which stood in the way of perfect production, viz., the liability of some clays to crack more than others. They succeeded in fixing a definite scale of their respective qualities, and arranged them according to their order of merit, under the name of "cracking clays;" they also proved that some of the waters then indiscriminately used were unfit for potting purposes, and that many accidents were attributable to carelessness on this point. All these studies and many more were very beneficial to the trade in general; and consequently, when their struggles were over, and all their difficulties had been surmounted, potting underwent a great change. Systematic rules were henceforth adhered to, by which risks were lessened, and, as a matter of course, profits largely increased. Their cream-colour was considered excellent, and they exported it to foreign parts in hitherto unprecedented quantities.

Thomas Whieldon commenced business prior to 1740 at Fenton Low, in a small thatched pot works which was destined gradually to expand into one of the most important manufactories of the time. His business was at first of a very modest sort. Carrying his samples in a bundle strapped to his back, he used to walk from one town to another canvassing for orders. He made small fancy articles for hardware men, snuff-boxes that were mounted in metal at Birmingham, and Agate-ware knife-hafts for the Sheffield cutlers. To these he soon added the manufacture of table and tea-ware, mostly tortoiseshell, for which he acquired such a reputation that all the numerous specimens of his style, although made by a crowd of imitators, have since been known under the name of *Whieldon* ware.

As his connection increased, he built, in 1749, large additions to his works. Mr. L. Jewitt *(Life of Josiah Wedgwood)* gives some interesting extracts from his account books, and several invoices which show us the sort of ware *Whieldon* commonly made. While other potters were pursuing a course which would have ruined the trade by underselling each other, and turning out a ware so coarse and clumsy that, notwithstanding its cheapness, it was on the eve of being abandoned by the public, *Whieldon* alone resisted this backward movement. Besides continuing the best traditions of his predecessors, and using the same processes in a perfected way, he brought out many ingenious novelties both in shapes and materials. He was assisted by the best model makers, and with great discrimination he selected his apprentices from amongst the most intelligent youths of the district. They profited so much by his tuition that nearly all of them were eminently successful in after life. *Josiah Spode*, *Robert Garner*, *J. Barker*, and *W. Greatbatch* all made a name for themselves in the Potteries. *Josiah Wedgwood* was then twenty-four years of age. He had just terminated his first partnership with *Harrison*, of Stoke, and it is to the credit of *Whieldon* that he was able to discern and appreciate the abilities of the young potter, and that he secured him as a partner for five years.

It would be very interesting to discover the share *Wedgwood* had in the production of *Whieldon's* most refined pieces. He was already expert in all the branches of the trade, including throwing, modelling, and the compositions of bodies and glazes. He spent much of his time in the first years of his partnership in making trials and preparing blocks and moulds, and it is not improbable that some of those delicate pickle trays, scalloped plates, perforated tea-pots of tortoiseshell or Agate-ware, now so highly prized, are the work of his own hands. More will be known about his doings at *Whieldon's;* documents of that period are not wanting, and many fresh ones may one day turn up and throw more light on the subject. We know already that it was he who compounded the bright green glaze, so much admired that it was the cause of many successful patterns, all designed to show it off to advantage. The cauliflower, pine-apple, and melon ware derived their charming effect from the green glaze contrasting with the cream-colour; while embossed pieces were mottled with green and yellow, others were covered all over with the green ground. But the tint of earthenware had in their hands become so white and pure, that the partners were proud of showing its quality, and frequently abstained from hiding it under the then fashionable coloured glazes.

They also made another kind of ware, in which the plain colour of the clay was reserved for the ground, while parts only of the reliefs were slightly touched up with a dash of brown, yellow, or green; sometimes a faint cloud of grey was thrown over the handles and spouts. These latter specimens are perhaps the most charming of all and mark the approaching end of the underglaze decoration, to which plain earthenware was soon to be preferred. When the partnership with *Wedgwood* came to an end, tradition, which represents *Whieldon* as a very prudent and cautious man, says that he was not sorry to part from his young associate, of whose daring and enterprising spirit he was rather afraid. Not wishing to embark in any other new-fangled enterprises, but being satisfied with making money as he had always done, they parted, some say even before the term of the partnership agreement had expired. We can hardly credit these statements when we see with what untiring energy *Whieldon* had so far endeavoured to advance his art, and steadily kept at the head of his contemporaries. By him the foreign trade was largely increased, and from his time Staffordshire ware was sent all over the world. Many of his pieces are still found in distant parts. Our friend, Dr. I. Lyons, of Hartford, U.S., has been able to form a collection of tortoiseshell, cauliflower, and other varieties of the time, with specimens picked up in the cottages of Connecticut. Near the place where once stood his thatched pot works, *Whieldon* built for himself a large and elegant house, which is still standing, and where he died in 1798, at a very advanced age.

No sooner had the manipulative and other processes reached the point at which it was difficult, if not impossible, to further improve upon them, than the potter turned his attention to a selection of the models best calculated to bring out all their qualities. The tortoiseshell-ware, with its variety of colours, lent itself to all sorts of combinations, and a special treatment was required for the modelling of the pieces intended to be so decorated. The old potter was generally his own modeller; and none was better qualified than the practical man to contrive a design adapted to the means at his disposal. He cared little for imitating the works of other people or other countries, but consulting only his own taste, and profiting by the efforts of his fellow-workers, his style was rational and genuine, being, above all, appropriate to the ways and means by which it was to be produced.

While *Whieldon* was carrying out the latest improvements in earthenware, a decided tendency towards fancy shapes and the picturesque in ornamentation began to show itself even in the most ordinary pieces. A tea-pot assumed the look of an attractive and dainty little toy, and we hear of the gallants of London offering to their lady-loves pretty tea-pots of Staffordshire ware. The hackneyed ornaments which had been handed down from father to son were discarded by the rising generation, and new ideas as well as new men came to the front. Leaves and fruits were the inexhaustible stock from which the artist drew at first most of his inspirations. A pickle tray was formed with a common leaf, delicately marked with all its veining, and glazed with its natural colour; while in the centre a few buds and flowers were symmetrically disposed for the purpose of securing a variety of tints. A fruit—the pine-apple for instance—was transformed into a jug or a cup; the upper part, with its lozenge-shaped imbrications, received the yellow glaze they knew so well how to make rich and bright, while their dark green glaze seemed especially intended to reproduce the vivid colour of the pointed leaves ornamentally arranged underneath. The same notions, applied to the reproduction of a melon resting on its leaf, inaugurated another style of ware. Treated in various ways, the pieces upon which this fruit was introduced all went by the name of melon-ware, and so were styled also the generality of pieces mottled green and yellow. From the imitation of common fruits and vegetables the potters derived their most successful patterns.

Cauliflower-ware was manufactured in enormous quantities, and in many sizes and shapes. Its novelty and originality remain striking even to our day. The potters took a just pride in the perfection of their cream-colour body and their green glaze. Nothing simpler could have been devised to bring out their quality and contrast them together. How well the one comes in to represent the flowers with their smooth embossments and their thousands of minute dots, and the other to cover with a mellow and powerful colour the net-work of sunk and raised lines that veins the curled leaves! The execution is as simple and forcible as the idea. It has just the amount of conventional treatment that a work of art demands to become a "Type." There are many more pretentious pieces which have fewer claims to be spoken of in the same way.

Fancy, cramped a little by the requirements of table-ware, found an unlimited scope for its display in the merely ornamental articles that were already in demand; quaintly modelled by local artists, and made pleasant with the brightest hues of underglaze colour, all sorts of household and toy pieces were made; strange birds, curious animals, hippopotami and elephants, hanging vases bearing a large sunflower, which would have delighted the modern æsthete, flower vases for the decoration of the mantel-piece, even small figures, soldiers, workmen of different trades, and busts or medallions of the king and queen, and of the worthies of the day. We must also mention the wares made in imitation of Chinese porcelain; although they purport to be decorated with apple blossoms and mandarins, they are rather original fancies derived from a curious style imperfectly remembered, than the actual copy of any particular piece. Upon them all the English hand is easily traceable. Some are perforated and cut out all over the surface, exhibiting an unusual amount of ingenuity and skill, and must once have been considered marvels of workmanship.

Of all these, many identical replicas are still to be met with; it is to be borne in mind that as yet painting, which can indefinitely vary the aspect of the same piece, had not come to the potter's assistance; moulded shapes and raised decorations were alone resorted to, and the effect could merely be diversified by the stains of the mottled glazes.

It is somewhat provoking, when we know most of the names of the tortoiseshell potters, to be unable to ascribe accurately to any of them the different specimens that we value and admire; no marks ever appear to help us, and none ever thought of following the practice of *Toft* by signing their best works. Artistic property was in no way protected, perhaps not even acknowledged; as soon as a model enjoyed a run of success, it was at once taken up by a crowd of imitators. *Whieldon* used to bury his imperfect pieces, lest they should be picked up and copied, but it was an ineffectual precaution after all, and his happiest novelties soon fell a prey to the plagiarist. Pirating other's ideas and shapes was considered almost legitimate; we know that later on many manufacturers thrived upon designs borrowed from *Wedgwood's* productions; the poor struggling potter who could not keep a modeller depended for his forms upon the unasked assistance of his wealthier brethren, in the same manner as a workman who in our days sets up in a small way of business on his own account, asks a neighbour for the loan of his blocks to make moulds from.

We can only distinguish the early pieces from those made long afterwards in the old moulds, by their being cast instead of pressed, and thereby being much thinner in the substance. Impressed in terra-cotta moulds, the ornaments are neater and sharper, the thick glaze is of a deeper tint, and the colours run more freely. Some are stamped with seals like the "Salt-glaze," and partly made by hand; all of them are "potted" with a skill and care often wanting in more modern productions.

Painting on cream-colour, which was soon to be so generally practised, was only introduced when the body had been made white enough to resemble china more closely. This whitening was obtained by the mixing of a small quantity of zaffre with the glaze; and this innovation, continued to our time, was due to *Aaron Wedgwood* and *William Littler*, who were also the first to glaze their ware by immersion. Certain portions of the glaze, the clay which composed the body of the pottery, and a small quantity of zaffre were mixed with water; in this liquid the vessels, when dry, were dipped, and absorbing the water, received a thick coating of the ground materials in suspension.

Shortly after this, *Enoch Booth* began the practice of firing his ware before dipping it; we accept this on the testimony of Shaw, noticing at the same time that firing in biscuit was practised by all the makers of Delft-ware.

Towards 1750, *R. and T. Baddeley*, of Shelton, made the first attempts at blue painting under the glaze, and the process was adopted by all the other potters.

Enamelling on cream-colour was successfully carried on at the same period by *Mrs. Warburton*, who is credited with having, in 1751, made the last improvement in earthenware bodies; she acquired a great celebrity for her painting, and until 1769 she enamelled for *Josiah Wedgwood.*

Another enamel painter was *Warner Edwards*, of Hanley; he not only worked himself, but supplied the trade with colours of his own making. He died in 1753.

When painting came into fashion, few trained hands could be obtained in the Potteries; many were sent for from Holland, where there was a superabundance of clever men; this may in some measure account for the small degree of originality noticeable on the painted pieces, when compared with those modelled and embossed according to the traditional style of the old English potter; here we may incidentally remark that England was not the only country which borrowed her ceramic painters from abroad. In the records of the old Saint Lucas Guild, the Academy of Delft, to which the best faïence decorators were affiliated, most of the names inscribed as members, as far back as 1645, are those of foreigners who had come from France and Italy.

From this time pottery will lower itself into becoming the humble retainer of aristocratic porcelain; the body will try to ape the whiteness of its prototype, if not its transparency; blue painting will adopt the Worcester style, and enamel decoration will emulate the works of Bow and Chelsea, and thus become a second-hand imitation of Oriental china. The lead-glaze and the smooth surface of the cream-colour were perfectly adapted to kiln painting, and this sort of decoration was at first fairly used, but as it could only by its cheapness compete with the china it was intended to replace, nothing of importance was ever attempted. A bright iron red was often used alone or relieved with a few touches of varied colours; Dutch landscapes or grotesque scenes were sometimes freely sketched, and groups of flowers were painted with bright enamels in a conventional manner. However, as pieces of this sort generally belong to the second half of the 18th century, they hardly come within our scope, and we shall not linger on the subject; let it suffice to say that the style of painting was gradually simplified, and the transition can easily be traced from the over-decorated pieces to the plain earthenware, merely edged with a brown or blue line, that was soon to come into fashion.

Meanwhile, the tortoiseshell-ware continued to be made, but the best efforts were brought to bear upon the new bodies, and it was losing some of its primitive character; the peculiar carving of blocks and "pitcher" moulds and the engraving of ornament sunk in the hollow were given up as being too slow and expensive, when the introduction of plaster of Paris gave facilities for casting moulds at a trifling cost upon any model whatsoever, whether it be a piece of metal, china, or wood carving, little regard being paid to its fitness for reproduction in clay. Though the advantageous properties of plaster, its capability of taking an impression, and its porous texture which so rapidly absorbs the water, had been known for a long time previously in the Potteries, it was utilized but at a comparatively late period. A cream-colour tea-pot in the Liverpool Museum, with an embossed barley pattern, has an inscription scratched on the bottom, stating that this was the first tea-pot ever pressed, dated and signed "J. Hollingshead, 175..." The simple and well-adapted types created in the locality gave way to more ambitious models ordered from sculptors in London, who had never before thought of applying their talent to this new purpose. Tea-pots and jugs began to assume rustic and ultra-picturesque decorations, and to depart widely from geometrical and rational shapes.

We do not mean to say that fine and interesting pieces are not to be found amongst those resulting from this transformation of the Potter's style of modelling. The old man with short legs and ample waistcoat, whose cocked hat has been turned into use for a spout—the figure which constitutes the traditional Toby jug—evinces a quaint spirit of originality. Some groups were admirably modelled, and with a genuine sense of humour. The Sexton and the Parson going home arm in arm after a late supper; the Vicar asleep in his pulpit, while from underneath Moses vainly endeavours to prompt him with the next sentence of his sermon; the *Voyez* jug, with the huntsman and the milkmaid, of which Dr. Diamond has an example coloured with the most harmonious combinations of tortoiseshell glazes—these, and many others of the same kind, though of a date that brings them near to our own time, were still done with the old cream-colour, and stained with the softly-mottled colours used by *Whieldon*. All these are very different from the clumsy comicalities, made afterwards with white ware coloured on the surface, which are known by the name of Staffordshire figures.

In our judgment, an absolute line of demarcation separates the productions of an art which kept steadfastly advancing in an original path, free from the intrusions of foreign notions, from those of a more complex style, the fruit of studies often incomplete or ill-understood, and which admits of an admixture of totally irrelevant elements. When, for instance, we are pleased with the best pieces of English salt-glaze or tortoiseshell, we never think of comparing them with any pieces belonging to another nation; they stand apart, and are to be taken as they are; they may at least be considered as the highest expression of a genuine taste, the development of which we can trace from its most uncouth and inexperienced early attempts. We feel a sense of disappointment and even of annoyance when we detect signs of a natural feeling having been perverted by extraneous teaching. Acanthus leaves are ill at ease on a Staffordshire tea-pot, and we are disheartened when we recognise upon the features of an otherwise coarse and vulgar figure a faint likeness to the Greek nose and the eye of Apollo. In one case we have a standard steadily advancing, in the other we have a descent savouring slightly of caricature.

But we are overstepping the bounds of our subject. It is not our purpose to follow the transformations of the Potter's art after the middle of the 18th century, the close of the epoch to which our investigations are limited. We must now briefly say that since that time earthenware pottery has thrived and flourished under the hands of innumerable skilful manufacturers, and rapidly become the staple trade of all the English pottery-producing centres, from which it has spread to many places on the Continent, and even to the United States. A list of all those who had a hand in its improvement would be endless, as also would an enumeration of the places where it has been manufactured since 1750.

The limits we have thus imposed upon ourselves put beyond our range the admirable works of the greatest potter of England, *Josiah Wedgwood.* Of his innumerable achievements it would be unbecoming to speak in an inadequate manner, and his life must be read in the exhaustive books which have been devoted to his memory. For the same reason are we precluded from speaking of the earthenware of Liverpool, where almost all descriptions of Pottery were manufactured; of the cream-colour of Leeds, which equalled, if it did not surpass, the finest ware previously made at any other place; and of a host of Potters established all over the kingdom, whose names are mentioned and productions described in the works written on the subject. Many interesting discoveries must be passed over. We should like to relate how the transfer of a black print to the surface of a glazed piece gave rise to a new mode of decoration; how, shortly afterwards, under-glaze printing superseded painting in blue, and a bright and complicated pattern being thus obtainable at a small cost, a revolution was accomplished in the decoration of earthenware; but, however enticing the subject, we cannot attempt to treat of it here.

Our account has come to an end; the old English Potter, with his quaint ways, is replaced by the educated manufacturer with eclectic taste, but he owes much to the intelligence and energy with which his modest forerunners prepared the way for the excellence now attained to. If this imperfect essay help to bring to light their merits and originality, and if it be accepted as a small tribute to the memory of these neglected workmen and artists, who in their secluded pot works were once exerting their ingenuity, and who bequeathed to us the fruits of their labours, the writer's most earnest hopes will have been realised, and his little effort will not have been made in vain.

DESCRIPTION

OF THE

PLATES.

Pl. I.

EARLY BRITISH URN.

PLATE I.

EARLY BRITISH URN.

HEIGHT $5\frac{1}{2}$ INCHES.

THE researches of antiquaries have brought to light a large quantity of the earthen utensils used by the Early Britons; urns and pitchers have been discovered in most of the grave mounds and hut circles that have been excavated all over the kingdom; but beyond the statement that they belong to a very remote antiquity, no precise information is to be found as to the date of their production; they have up to this time been classed under the convenient heading of "Pre-historic Pottery." They are the work of the native tribes of the British Isles; we know that they were made long before the Roman occupation, but we may also surmise that the tradition was kept up after the conquest by Cæsar; so, there may be a great difference between the ages of similar specimens. The clay with which they were formed, sometimes coarse and mixed with pebbles, but in other instances more finely prepared, has been taken as affording a possible though doubtful clue to their respective ages. Sun-dried or imperfectly fired, they present a strange likeness to the primitive pottery of many distant countries, and in some cases they recall the vessels kneaded and shaped by women amongst the savages of the new world.

In the barrows of Great Britain votive vases are found associated with human remains, whether cremation had or had not been resorted to; they vary somewhat in detail, according to localities, but they show everywhere, whatever their size may be, a similarity of shape and decoration, the ornament consisting of incised lines and punctures. The more usual form is that of an urn with expanded mouth, not turned but rounded by hand, and occasionally finished off with small handles or loops for the purpose of suspension. The work does not exhibit traces of any tool but a sharpened bone or a rough nail. From their probable uses they have been arranged into four classes :— Cinerary urns, drinking cups, food vessels, and incense cups. The bones and ashes found in the first-named leave no doubt as to their employment; the three other classes have perhaps been named somewhat on speculation. Much knowledge is to be gathered about Celtic pottery by the study of the works of Bateman, Sir John Lubbock, Dr. Birch, and others.

We give one specimen of the ware to represent the ordinary style of its decoration. By its shape it could be classified with the cinerary urns, but it was found at Meigle in a stone cist by the side of a skeleton; cremation had not been practised, and the vase is of hard clay, sun-dried but not fired. It was formerly in the collection of Dr. Barnard Davis.

Pl. II.

E F

A H

G

B C D

MEDIÆVAL WARE.

PLATE II.

MEDIÆVAL WARE.

E give in this plate a selection of some of the more characteristic shapes of Early English ware. Most of these specimens have been dug out in London or in the Potteries district, at a depth varying from six feet to twelve feet, and may be considered as genuine representatives of the productions of the time. Chaffers, in his interesting work upon mediæval earthenware vessels, explains how hopelessly one would endeavour to appropriate these homely utensils to any particular era between the 7th and 15th centuries, a period to which they may be said to belong by their particular forms. We shall follow his example by classifying together such pieces as were made before the series of improvements commenced in England towards the middle of the 16th century. All those represented here are roughly thrown, the handles are all made by hand, and the spouts pinched into form with the fingers; the feet exhibit in many cases a sort of fluting, produced by pressure of the thumb, a peculiarity which, by-the-bye, is likewise noticed upon Early German pieces.

A. An early jug of yellow clay found in Farringdon Street. The top part is covered with a dull green glaze. Having been made on the whirler and not thrown on the wheel, it is hardly round in shape. The ware not having been protected by saggers, stuck in the firing to the next piece, and the place has been tinted with the green glaze with which the latter was covered, a fact which led to the supposition that all blemishes were covered with a spot of glaze.

B. Found in Lombard Street. A pot of red clay partially glazed with lead. The inside presents the peculiarity of being washed over with light yellowish clay, and the handle is thumb-marked in a conspicuous manner.

C. A small drinking cup of buff clay coated inside with green glaze. In shape and material it bears a striking likeness to some old Roman pieces.

D. An ale mug of grey Stone-ware, with the curled work on the foot. It was found in London, but strangely enough we possess a similar piece dug up in the Potteries.

E. A tyg with two handles placed on the same side, probably one of the earliest Staffordshire tygs, made of red brick clay, and covered over with dark brown glaze.

F. A jug of Norman shape, as figured in the MSS. of the period; light grey Stone-ware highly fired, and sounding like metal, very superior in make to the pottery of after times. The foot has the usual curl produced by the thumb, and the lower part of the body is also thumb-marked in the same manner as some old Roman ware. Although all the above pieces were found in London, it still remains a matter of doubt whether they were made by local potters, or by some of the foreign workmen who settled early in England, and there produced articles similar to those made on the Continent, or whether they are merely importations from Germany.

G and **H** are two varieties of brown jugs found in the Potteries. On the second example the two handles are placed on opposite sides.

Pl. III.

EARLY PUZZLE JUGS.

PLATE III.

EARLY PUZZLE JUGS.

HEIGHT 7½ INCHES.

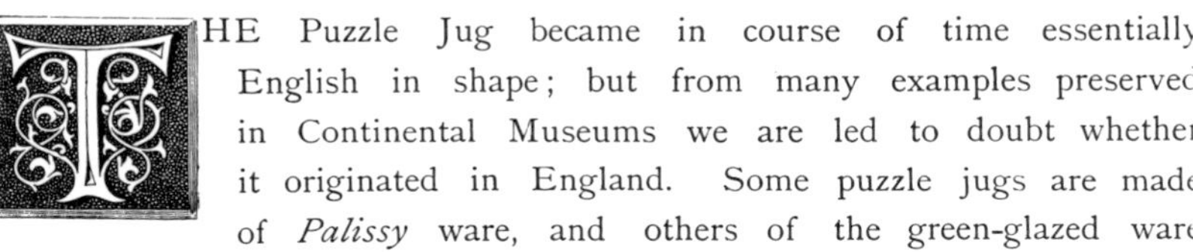

THE Puzzle Jug became in course of time essentially English in shape; but from many examples preserved in Continental Museums we are led to doubt whether it originated in England. Some puzzle jugs are made of *Palissy* ware, and others of the green-glazed ware of Nuremberg. The Puzzle afforded matter for a joke amongst drinkers. A hollow rim furnished with spouts communicates with a pipe, which, passing through the handle, goes down to the bottom of the jug. The liquor can be sucked out from one of the spouts, by taking the precaution of stopping with the thumb the little air hole pierced under the handle. The trick was considered a good one for a very long time, since Puzzle Jugs continued to be manufactured for more than two centuries. The first on the plate is dated 1571, one of the earliest dates recorded upon any English piece, though it by no means follows that others were not made before that time. The figures are not laid on in slip, but raised in clay. It was formerly in Mr. Bohn's collection. The other one, which belonged to Mr. Peter Norton, is slightly different in shape, and notched about with a square tool. This way of enhancing the effect of colours upon a flat surface was subsequently employed upon the green-glazed ware of the end of the 18th century. Both jugs are covered with the same dull green glaze used by the Romans, and found on the earliest mediæval pieces. This glaze was probably handed down from the Romans to their successors, and its use was never discontinued.

STONE-WARE MUGS.

PL. IV.

PLATE IV.

STONE-WARE MUGS.

HEIGHT 9 INCHES.

ROM the resemblance they bear to many identified pieces, we should not hesitate in ascribing these mugs to Fulham. The first is of the brown granulated Stone-ware peculiar to the specimens found along the banks of the Thames, inscribed with the names of well-known public houses, or of private persons living in the neighbourhood. This one was formerly in the collection of the Rev. W. Sibthorpe. Its decoration is not, perhaps, highly artistic, but it is clearly a speaking pottery, and without the aid of any inscription, he for whom the mug was intended would readily understand what the potter had to say. The sportsman, who has had a hot day of it over the moors with his dogs and gun, comes to rest on the inn's bench, and after having quaffed a bumper of the cooling beer, may like to have the incidents of the day brought back to his mind. Here they are on his tankard in a graphic form: the sun that made his march so laborious; the scattered trees, under the scanty shade of which he enjoyed a short halt; the flying game; the dogs so like his own, that he could call them each by his name; he himself, portrayed on horseback, holding in his hand that whip, the importance of which is expressed by its exaggerated size; and last, though not least, for fear he should be so ungrateful as to forget the hospitable roof under which he is so pleasantly welcomed, the very inn where he enjoys himself so thoroughly, and where it is hoped he will often return to rest himself again. Sometimes a memorable sporting event is recorded in an inscription incised in the clay. Thus we have seen the following lines on a mug of similar character: "On Bansted down a hare Was found which led (us) a smoking round. Abraham Hamman, Sussex, 1725." The other mug is made of grey ware, partially coloured with brown. The decoration carries also with it a special meaning. In the centre, supported by two beef-eaters, is a medallion of Queen Anne, but the portrait was not sufficiently life-like to permit of dispensing with an inscription, and so we read: "*Drink to the pious memory of good Queen Anne*, 1729." As the date is 19 years posterior to the death of the Queen, we may conjecture that the mug was made for an old servant proud of his loyalty to his late sovereign; the potter knew that nothing could please him more than a gift bearing such an inscription. One can realise the feeling of the old toper, when, drinking a convivial draught out of his favourite mug, he could take the opportunity to discourse with his friends about his past services, and what they remembered of the good old times. The pack of dogs is in this instance again running at the bottom; there is hardly a piece of Stone-ware where they are not seen, even on those made in our days.

STONE-WARE BEAR.

PLATE V.

STONE-WARE BEAR.

HEIGHT 12 INCHES.

E all remember the Bradwardine Bear in Walter Scott's *Antiquary;* it was a vessel peculiar in shape to the old English Squire as the glass or silver boot was to the German Landgrave. Was not the good Briton readier for a laugh and a joke when he had emptied the comical head of the bear, whose uncouth body contained the foaming beer, than when his drink was poured out for him from a common-place jug of stiff and classical shape, at the sight of which he felt bound to assume a dignified and formal countenance? This one is grim and shaggy enough to put his children to flight, and no doubt its former owner often revelled in its appearance on the table. Its black rough coat is made of minute shavings of clay, and its eyes and claws of shining white paste. Nottingham was once celebrated for jugs of this sort; and at Congleton, in Cheshire, nicknamed the Bear's Town, on account of the partiality of its inhabitants for bear-baiting, they were in great demand. The potters of Staffordshire used to send a great number there, made of white Stone-ware decorated with brown slip, or of common Earthenware. One made in the beginning of this century represented a Russian bear crushing between its paws a diminutive Bonaparte.

PL. VI.

SLIP DISH.

PLATE VI.

SLIP DISH.

DIAMETER 16½ INCHES.

NOTHING is known about *Thomas Toft* beyond what we have related in another place. The huge platters he signed are so numerous that the generic name of Toft dishes has been accepted for all the Slip-decorated ones made in his time. This represents a gentleman in the costume of Charles II.'s reign, in the act of drinking a toast; he has the plumed hat of the cavalier, but no sword. The outline is traced with brown slip punctuated with white dots; the interspaces are filled in with orange colour; three flowers, a distant reminiscence of fleurs-de-lys, and a sort of uncouth garland complete the subject; on the broad rim, brown and orange slips have been trailed to form a close trellis work. The body of the dish is of coarse marl, washed on the inside with a coat of fine yellow clay; it is highly fired, very heavy and resistant. The whole is very effective, and if we consider the decoration only as a means of bringing out the contrast of colours, we may pass over the oddity of its execution. We have heard critics dismiss such pieces in a few words, to the effect that they are no better than the barbarous works of New Zealanders; but why this should not be taken as a compliment instead of condemnation we fail to perceive. We do not in any way despise the carvings of the clubs and canoe heads of the savage; they exhibit a real understanding of what can make them rich and beautiful, and display a fanciful combination of lines and proportions that owes nothing to servile imitation. The archaic creations of the early Etruscans and Greeks contain in their roughness all the germs of what was one day to be the art of Praxiteles and Phidias, and this none the less for their being in some respects akin to the works of some Polynesian savages. Shall we pass an irrevocable sentence upon the old Slip Potter on account of his imperfections? At least his trials forcibly tell us about obsolete tastes and forgotten customs; they make us acquainted with the state of artistic education in his times, pottery in all ages reflecting the condition of every other branch of art; we see how meritorious these old workmen were in following up unremittingly emendations and improvements, and how a genuine and even refined style was to be the result of their primitive and uncouth labours.

PL. VII.

TYG.

PLATE VII.

BROWN TYG.

HEIGHT 6¾ INCHES.

N indefinite number of handles applied to a large cup of coarse clay distinguishes the *Tyg* from other vessels of early times. Drinking cups furnished in that manner were manufactured at Wrotham, and in several other places in England, but the term *Tyg* does not seem to have been used out of the Staffordshire Potteries district. It is probably a corruption in the local dialect from the Roman word *Tegula*, a tile, a word which in Italian has become *Tegola*, in Spanish *Teja*, in old German *Tieghel*, in French *Tuile*, etc. Bosworth, in his "Anglo-Saxon Dictionary," gives the name *Tigel*, a tile, a brick, anything made of clay, a pot, a vessel. Posset and other compound drinks were brewed in the *Tyg* at social gatherings. It stood in the middle of the table, and each guest helped himself to its contents; in its use it was not unlike the Greek *crater*, a capacious vase containing a mixed beverage, out of which a slave filled the cups all round; but as slaves did not wait at old English convivial meetings, the common cup was provided all round with convenient handles, in order that each guest could draw it to himself. Cups or glasses were dispensed with, every one drinking from the pot. A curious passage in *William of Malmesbury* says, "Formerly the vessels were regularly divided for to prevent quarrels. King Edgard commanded the drinking vessels to be made with knobs in the inside at certain distance from each other, and decreted that no person, under a certain penalty, should either himself drink or compel another to drink at one draught more than from one of these knobs to the other."

The handles and other applied parts were made by hand with twisted and crumpled bits of clay, much in the same fashion as those on the old British glass found in the barrows; there is the same disposition and the same treatment. A Tyg bears a striking likeness to an Anglo-Saxon drinking cup.

A strange and no doubt fortuitous analogy is also to be traced with many ancient Spanish glass cups, which are shaped and decorated exactly in the same manner.

The Tyg reproduced in this plate is of the common red clay, coated with manganese, which under the name of "*magnus*" was beginning to be employed for making a deeper black than the one previously obtained with oxide of iron. It is inscribed in yellow slip, "*Margret Colley, 1684.*" Not a dot of slip appears on the piece besides the inscription; all the interest lies in the four double handles, and the notched strips of clay, which, without taking away any of the simplicity of the shape, are sufficient to make of it an unusual work fit for presentation. Like nearly all primitive productions it has a grand character as to form and the glaze shines brilliantly on the sharp edges of the hand-work. It was found in an old cottage in Stoke, and had been preserved up to this time in the same family, together with sundry other pieces of old ware. In this case there is no doubt about the inscribed name having reference to the person for whom the piece was intended, and not to the maker.

PL. VIII.

TYG.

PLATE VIII.

TYG.

HEIGHT 7 INCHES.

BROWN and yellow Tyg of the late period. The handles have no longer the same importance as on the early specimens. This is one of the most forcible examples illustrating the process of Slip-decoration. Like all similar productions of the time, it is made of coarse grey marl, washed over in the inside and on the top part with a coat of fine yellow clay; the bottom is covered with a mixture of red clay and manganese; upon these grounds the same slips have been used, dark upon light and light upon dark, to trace the decoration. The Tyg has four handles, and is inscribed "*Mary Shiffilbottom, 1705.*" The potter who spelt in this way the old name of Shufflebottom was certainly not a scholar, but considering the state of education at that time, we may be astonished that the posset pot maker of Staffordshire could even write at all. We may notice that most of the inscribed drinking cups were presented to ladies. We should not dare to hazard the supposition that this was on account of a well-known partiality of the fair sex for hot liquors; let us rather say that these Tygs were more an object of adornment for the shelves of the housewife than for utility, and were only taken down on very special occasions. That is perhaps why so many have been preserved to us, which otherwise would have disappeared like pieces in common use, now become so scarce; handed down from father to son as a sort of heirloom, they have thus escaped destruction. This specimen presents great similarities to the *Myers* cup of the Liverpool Museum, and to some pieces in Mr. Willett's collection, all of which seem to be the work of the same hand. It was found not long since in the Potteries.

PL. IX.

TYG.

PLATE IX.

TYG.

HEIGHT 9 INCHES.

HIS Tyg differs in many particulars from those made in Staffordshire. It is of a bright red colour, and the yellow slip with which it is decorated is stamped over with stars and rosettes, by means of a stick cut on its flat end into a geometrical pattern; besides, the light clay is in places coloured with copper green. These characteristics are seldom, if ever, found on the old Burslem pieces. The shape is also more complicated; from the lid and the six handles project an unusual number of knobs; a pipe passes through one of the handles, and communicates inside with a hole pierced at the bottom of the pot, in such a manner that the liquor can be sucked out through a little hole on the top. At Wrotham, in Kent, pieces of the same red clay, and bearing a decoration of an identical character, were extensively made at the time; so we feel inclined to ascribe this one to that manufacture. The ware made there was of a highly ornamental sort, and was often inscribed with the name of the place, but little is known about the potters who worked there. Chaffers gives *Jull* as the name of one of them, and the site of his manufactory is known to have belonged to the author of "John Evelyn's Diary." Antiquaries have as yet taken little trouble to gather documents concerning the productions of Wrotham, as has been done for the Staffordshire Potteries. It may be accounted for in this way, that the facts connected with a manufacture which was to disappear completely after so promising a start are less interesting to historians than those which refer to a district where the same industry slowly advanced year by year through a course of improvements until it had reached its present high state of excellence.

This piece is inscribed "*John Hugh*," probably the name of the possessor, and is dated 1690; it was formerly in the collection of the Rev. W. Sibthorp, of Nottingham; when that collection was dispersed, it passed into our hands for a modest sum. We take this occasion to express our astonishment at the little competition there is amongst English collectors for the possession of rare and curious specimens made in their own country. The highest prices we know of are those realised at the Bernal sale for the two wonderful Tygs now in the British Museum, £6 and £10 respectively. The figures are modest enough when compared with the money given for Continental faïence.

Pl. X.

PUZZLE JUG.

PLATE X.

BROWN PUZZLE JUG.

HEIGHT $7\frac{3}{4}$ INCHES.

THIS shows one of the many varieties of Puzzle Jugs. Here seven nozzles have been set upright on the rim, six having to be stopped with the fingers before any liquor can be sucked out from the seventh. The body is of a peculiar dark brown, sprinkled with minute yellow specks, probably dust of sagger clay, which makes it look like aventurine. Coarse as to shape, it is exceedingly rich in colour; the glaze is of the usual thick and treacly sort. It was formerly in Mr. Lucas' collection. We have, unfortunately, no voucher for its date, but we think it belongs to the latter part of the 17th century. There has always been in England a marked partiality for black ware; and although it was manufactured in many places on the Continent, nowhere does it seem to have so well suited the public taste as in this country. From the first trials made by the *Elers* in the dry bodies, and the black glazed Tygs of Staffordshire, the ware was constantly made and improved upon, until it became the black basalt of *Josiah Wedgwood*, and since his time the manufacture has never been discontinued.

Another shape of Puzzle Jug is shown in the background. It is of a light brown colour, and offers nothing particular beyond its unusual flat form. On the other side is a large brown mug, which has a thick coating of white clay scratched in with horizontal and transverse lines by the same process for which *Shaw*, of Burslem, took out a patent in 1735; but whether it is a piece of his make or not we are unable to say.

Pl. XI.

Posset Pot.

PLATE XI.

POSSET POT.

HEIGHT 9½ INCHES.

TYGS disappeared completely when the use of earthenware became more general, and mugs or other vessels were manufactured in bulk for the table. The intercourse, created by the increase of trade, between the people of Staffordshire and those of the neighbouring counties drove the local custom away. Loving cups, that is, large cups having one handle on each side, were still made in tortoiseshell or salt-glaze ware, and upon them the workman displayed his greatest skill; but as early as the beginning of the 18th century he abandoned the numberless combinations of handles which he had been so proud of setting round his favourite pieces. The custom of every guest drinking an honoured toast out of the same cup did not pass away altogether, but the vessel was no longer made in a style recalling that especial purpose. As we may see by this Posset Pot, the traditional form was altered into one resembling the Delft caudle pots, made at Lambeth, or imported from Holland. It is covered with a lid, and a spout has been placed on each side by which the liquor can be poured out into the drinking mugs. The clay used, the making of the piece, and the style of decoration, are precisely like those of the Tygs, but it is no longer the genuine old vessel of Staffordshire, and if it were not for the inscription all character would be lost. "*The best is not too good*," is written round the top in the usual black slip letters, studded over with yellow dots, and underneath are two initials, "H. L.," and the date "1714." We are in doubt as to the true meaning of the motto. Was it that, even at that date, the delicate and refined *Elers* ware was still so little known that this Posset Pot, with its rough decoration of slip, was considered as one of the best possible works in clay, or did it only allude to the quality of the mixtures brewed in it? For those who take an interest in the vicissitudes of such curiosities we shall add that it was discovered in a cottage, where it was used to keep flowers in on the window sill.

HEXAGONAL SLIP DISH.

PLATE XII.

HEXAGONAL SLIP DISH.

DIAMETER 13¼ INCHES.

HIS is a somewhat puzzling piece. The hexagonal shape is as much out of the ordinary way as the ornamentation traced upon it. The pomegranate, the well-formed fleur-de-lys, and the shield in the centre, are so seldom seen on ware of this sort that we cannot ascribe it to any particular place. It was found in Wales, but this gives us no clue, for to our knowledge three more specimens of the same dish have been found in far distant localities. We may surmise it was made in the South of England by some potter who used to visit the capital, where what he saw suggested to him the design of his plates, evidently borrowed from some foreign model. The raised outlines have again been obtained with a graven mould, and the intervals filled in with Slip. It bears the monogram "J. S.," probably the maker's.

PL. XIII.

SLIP JUG.

PLATE XIII.

SLIP JUG.

Height 9 Inches.

UGS decorated with slip are seldom met with; not that they were rarely made, but probably because, being of a more handy shape than a Tyg or an ornamental dish, they shared the fate of all crockery in common use, and were soon destroyed. The one represented on this plate was no doubt a presentation piece; it is an imitation of *T. Toft's* style, if not a work of his own hand. The clay and slips are the same as those of the dishes, and the brown outline was dotted over with the customary white specks; on each side a bird, perhaps meant for a peacock, is perched upon a branch, and the monogram "A. S.," with the date, "1704," is inscribed on the neck. Not much value seems ever to have been put upon such jugs, or the mugs that are sometimes found; they were never, as was the custom in the South of England, mounted with pewter, or mentioned in any document. However carefully finished a special piece, it was always considered as one of the common productions of the place. A fine brown jug in the Hanley Museum, dated 1690, is not only decorated with slip, but also with applied parts modelled by hand, a curious figure of Plenty on the front, and notched strips of clay on the sides, recalling the decorations of the Tygs.

Pl. XIV.

Slip Dish.

PLATE XIV.

SLIP DISH.

DIAMETER 14 INCHES.

ROYALTY is again the subject of this dish. A portrait of a King, George I. or George II., occupies the centre, and is surrounded with a deer and two birds, emblematic of hunting, one of the Royal prerogatives. The materials are the same as those of the early dishes, but the off-hand execution of their slip traceries has given place to a process which provides against any mistakes being made in the pouring out of the colour through a quill. There is no more improvisation of the design; on the mould upon which the bat of clay was formed into a platter, the outlines of the figures were deeply sunk, to be reproduced in relief on the piece; and to avoid harshness they were transversely cut with minute strokes, making facets which caught and reflected the light. On such a form many similar pieces could be pressed, while the work of the decorator consisted merely in painting the two coloured slips in the cavities prepared to receive them, a process which, by the bye, has some analogy to enamelling on copper. The head is no longer traced with the conventional scroll that stands for the features of *T. Toft's* kings, but is evidently copied from some good portrait or engraving. This is certainly a step in advance, but the picture adds little to the merit of the work, which consists in the richness of the glaze and the deep tone of the various slips. These pieces are rarely to be met with. Whenever we come across some of them amongst other kinds of ware, they catch the eye and claim attention by the striking and unusual scale of harmony of colour; we should advise those who have not yet noticed it to try the experiment. They look old and strange enough by the side of the more customary contents of the collections, like specimens of an art quite fresh and unknown, and will hold their own for effectiveness wherever they may stand. The notches impressed on the edges answered a double purpose; they are ornamental, and were intended to prevent the dish, which was fired face downwards, from sticking to the bat upon which it rested.

TYG.

PLATE XV.

TYG.

HEIGHT 9 INCHES.

QUAINT shape, evidently derived from some drinking glass of the period. It is one of the most curious amongst the great variety to be found in the shape of Tygs. The earliest ones were provided with only two handles placed closely together, so that two friends sitting on the same bench had each one side to drink from. Tygs were first of all straight and narrow, and the decoration consisted of applied pieces of light-coloured clay, stamped in separate moulds; subsequently they became shorter and more open at the mouth, and slip poured on the surface in fine traceries was alone used.

The number of handles was sometimes eight or even more, and each was double or triple; the shape sometimes concealed a curious contrivance like a whistle or a puzzle. The substance of this specimen is very coarse, and the trailings of slip are more clumsy than usual. It may probably have been made at Beckley. My friend, Dr. Thomas, of Llandudno, who presented it to me, found it near Chester. Two others nearly identical were also found in Cheshire; one of them is now in the Liverpool Museum; neither has any date or inscription.

CRADLES.

PLATE XVI.

CRADLES.

LENGTH 10 INCHES.

POTTERY is not only associated with the material necessities of man, but also with his feelings and affections, and has from the most ancient times been used to commemorate some momentous event in his career. An early British urn speaks to us of death and mysterious burial rites; a cradle of brown clay recalls the christening festivities in families of the Midland counties in the 17th century. The potter has always taken a pleasure in putting his best work into presents for his friends. In France, on the morning that followed the wedding, an *ecuelle*, or nicely decorated covered bowl with two handles, was always offered by the guests to the married couple. In England, on the occasion of the birth of a first child, a cradle made of clay or more precious material was presented to the parents; the custom has not died out altogether, for on a similar occurrence such a testimonial is presented by subscription to a man holding a public office. Sometimes the present took the form of an inscribed mug; but earthenware mugs and clay cradles are now out of fashion. By the number still to be found in Staffordshire, where these cradles were made, either of Slip-decorated ware, Salt-glaze, or Cream-colour, we may infer that presents of this sort were a tradition peculiar to the district. They were worked up in the plainest fashion; no moulds or models were required, and any workman could make them. Some flattened bats joined together sufficed for the shape, and knobs, rolled in the hands, were stuck at every corner by way of decoration. Some of them were afterwards ornamented with an inscription or a pattern of coloured slip. The first one given on this plate is coated over with red clay rudely incised and covered with manganese glaze; it is inscribed, "*Latron Wherecors, 1725. The gift is small but Love is all.*" The other, of a ware similar to the *Toft* dishes, has the name of "*Ralph Simpson.*" These are of a small size, but we possess several others of very large dimensions.

PL. XVII.

RED PUZZLE JUG.

PLATE XVII.

RED PUZZLE JUG.

HEIGHT 12 INCHES.

IKE the red Tyg, this piece cannot be attributed to Staffordshire, but must have been made either at Wrotham or at some other place in the South of England. It is a very strange shape—a ring with a tall neck and a high foot. The Owl Jugs in Mr. Willett's collection are made precisely in the same manner; on the bright red ground, yellow and red slips have been run together so as to form a marbling; the plain parts are incised with lines, but there is neither date nor inscription.

On the background are sketched a brown mug, with a lion deeply cut into the brown coating, showing the yellow clay of the body, and a money-box decorated with slip; on such money-boxes the old potter liked to display his humorous fancy. Upon this one a simple allegory is carried out by the representation of a hen and her chickens; the mother and the little ones, arrayed all round, are figured by twisted bits of clay, not much above the artistic manipulations of a pastry-cook; sometimes the piece is more complicated, and has several boxes set upon each other, each having a different sized hole at the bottom, to admit only of a certain coin dropping into each compartment.

PL. XVIII.

SLIP DISH.

PLATE XVIII.

SLIP DISH—GEORGE TAYLOR.

DIAMETER 16¾ INCHES.

PIECE of handiwork showing an individual taste, or a certain amount of skill, is always exceptionally valued in comparison with what has been done to a pattern. Hence it was that the old Slip dishes generally bore the name of the maker, who was proud to affix his signature to those unwonted proofs of his talent. Whether complete or imperfect, these works were equally admired by the possessor, who no doubt had never seen them surpassed; and as many are perforated for suspension, we may suppose they were kept as desirable ornaments, and not intended to be put to any practical use. When in course of time the process of casting and moulding permitted the reproduction of the same piece by the score, the potter did not think it worth while to sign them any longer; it was only as a safeguard against imposition, and as a necessity of the trade, that, many years later, *Josiah Wedgwood* thought of marking with his name the productions of his manufactory.

The subject represented on the Slip dishes were generally such as appealed to the imagination. Sometimes the decoration consisted of marvellous and hyperbolical flowers or monstrous animals, though more frequently preference was given to the figures of the King and his Queen, personages who in the minds of the simple inhabitants of the outlandish districts were looked upon as almost supernatural. In the same manner as the Italian artist exerted his fancy in designing the mythological god, the angels, or the saints, the potter of Staffordshire tried to represent royalty, of whom he formed a conception quite as confused and conventional. It would certainly be difficult to be less realistic than *George Taylor*, who signed this dish, has been in the treatment of his royal group. He has evidently endeavoured to emulate *Thomas Toft*; the decoration is, however, still more primitive, and it is clear that *Taylor's* loyalty was above his capacity as a draughtsman. His name is not mentioned amongst the potters of either Burslem or Hanley.

Pl. XIX.

COMBED-WARE.

PLATE XIX.

COMBED-WARE DISH.

DIAMETER 8½ INCHES.

Y this process most of the ware of the early Staffordshire potter was decorated; it was only in very especial circumstances that a piece was enriched with figures or flowers of trailed slip. While the ground was still in the wet state, lines of brown slip were poured upon the yellow clay, and then with a many-pointed tool, made of wire or leather, like those used by the wood grainer, they were combed down to imitate the veining of marble, and so an unlimited variety of effects was easily obtainable. An excavation seldom takes place at Hanley or Burslem without bringing to the surface heaps of fragments of this ware, but complete pieces are getting very scarce, and are, indeed, almost unobtainable; nearly all specimens now preserved by collectors have been dug out of the ground. Half a century ago ware of this kind was still commonly used by poor people, but it has now completely disappeared.

Upon the dish reproduced on this plate the comb has been first drawn downwards, and then in the opposite way, in such a manner as to make the indentations run into each other. On the small pipkin the marbling is performed all in the same direction, but it is varied by the handling of the comb. This is a pottery process quite peculiar to England. The transparency of the brown veining imparts to the coarsest piece a delicacy of detail and a deepness of tone which recalls a finely-streaked marble. This ware was the precursor of countless imitations of Agate and other hard stones; later on, four or five slips of different colours were poured on simultaneously, and were run in fanciful scrolls without being mixed with each other. In England, the surface marbling was brought to the highest degree of excellence; though different descriptions of mixed clays were also manufactured on the Continent, they never reached the same perfection.

PL. XX.

SLIP DISH.

PLATE XX.

SLIP DISH.

DIAMETER 14 INCHES.

OU are welcome to laugh at this grotesque performance of the jolly and funny old potter; the dish was never intended for aught but to induce a gentle merriment. Do not forget that the maker never anticipated that he was working for you or me, the sensitive and squeamish children of a refined century, and that he might one day have to undergo our criticism. The noble and solemn Greek interred his vases in stately tombs, foreseeing that in after ages they would come out, proclaiming the elevation of his thoughts and the splendour of his art. The rough workman of Staffordshire did his work on the spur of the moment; it was a morning's joke, destined to be forgotten by the evening. This may be one of the sarcastic presents customarily sent on St. Valentine's day. A neighbour's wife, or perhaps his own, had shown herself somewhat liable to the white sin of curiosity or interference, and to her the anonymous potter sends this cutting allegory. In the dish are depicted Lot's wife, two angels blowing trumpets, and the pillar of salt; and for fear that the intention should not be forcibly enough expressed, an inscription is added, "*Remember Lot's Wife*," with the date, "1727," to show that it was intended to relate to some particular occurrence. Scriptural jokes were freely indulged in between the period of the Reformation and the appearance of Methodism, which altered so much the manners of the people in the Potteries district.

The outlines of the subject have been graved on the pitcher form upon which the dish has been potted with the usual yellow clay, the cavities enclosed by the raised lines being afterwards filled in with black and red slip.

SCRATCHED-WARE JUG.

PLATE XXI.

SCRATCHED-WARE JUG.

HEIGHT 8½ INCHES.

ALTHOUGH the shape of this jug recalls the early ones, it is of a rather modern date, to judge from the doggerel verse scratched upon it; it is made of common brick clay, coated with yellow slip; the coating was scraped off with a tool so as to form a decoration—the sun on the front, a bird and flowers on one side, and on the other the following inscription:—

"COME FILL ME FULL WITH LIQUOR SWEET
FOR THAT IS GOOD WHEN FRIENDS DO MEET
BUT PRAY TAKE CARE DON'T LET ME FALL
LEAST YOU LIST YOUR LIQUOR JUG AND ALL.—
CATHERINE DAVIES AGED 8 YEARS."

The date has been obliterated by the person herself for whom the jug was made; when she became old she did not like to have her age so recorded, and therefore ground the figures off, so, at least, we were told by her grandchildren.

A jug decorated by the same process, in Mr. Willett's collection, is dated 1708.

PL. XXII.

ENGLISH DELFT.

PLATE XXII.

ENGLISH DELFT DISH.

DIAMETER 13 INCHES.

HERE is plenty of evidence that after William of Orange ascended the throne he endeavoured to foster in England the making of the ware of his own country; he patronised the Lambeth potters, and blue and white Delft tiles were soon largely employed for fire-places, shop windows, and wall decoration; at his suggestion a number of dishes were painted with the portraits of himself and the Queen, and these being lavishly distributed all over the country, spread his popularity. These dishes may have been made in every factory in England, judging from the unequal quality of their workmanship; some bear mere barbarous outlines of the king's features; others, on the contrary, are decorated with equestrian figures, cleverly drawn, or elaborate representations of the royal couple. The one we have selected for reproduction is, we think, unquestionably the work of an English hand; we cannot speak very highly of its style of decoration; the trees are daubed on with a sponge, and the colours are not over bright, but it has a look of genuineness about it which does not allow of the supposition that it was painted in Holland; it also presents the peculiarity, never occurring on Dutch pieces, of a back glazed with lead, instead of the stanniferous enamel that covers the inside. But whether made at Lambeth or at some other place where Delft ware was manufactured, we are unable to say; no marks have so far been found upon any of these dishes to help us to their identification.

The four small vases, with entwined handles, seen in front of the dish, are similar in shape to some pieces made of coarse clay decorated with Slip. The piece is called "a nest of cups," and may be considered as a form peculiar to the English potter. It has the thin pinkish glaze and the hard body of the sack bottles, and was probably made at the same time and at the same place, that is to say, many years before the William and Mary dishes.

PL. XXIII.

ENGLISH DELFT DISH.

PLATE XXIII.

ENGLISH DELFT DISH.

DIAMETER 13 INCHES.

E may well ask ourselves the puzzling question—What has become of the immense quantity of English Delft ware turned out at the twenty manufactories that at one time were working at Lambeth, and at the numerous pot works of Liverpool and Bristol, where for years it remained the staple trade of the town? In our days, it is with the greatest difficulty that we can pick up a few stray specimens of British make amongst the crowd of common pieces sent over by the Dutch exporters. In many cases we can only trust to the style of painting, and this is not always a safe guide, because many of those that bear a foreign design may have been made in England.

Little doubt need be entertained about this particular dish having been painted in England; in no way does it recall any of the continental ware by its very peculiar glaze, drawing, or colour; the inside is coated with a thin greenish enamel, and the back, glazed with lead, is tinted with tortoiseshell colours. The drawing in brown and blue of the group and accessory trees and foliage is most primitive, and, although executed with great care, does not show a hand long trained to this sort of painting; it looks like a piece on which a common workman has tried to surpass himself.

Eve's temptation was a subject frequently reproduced on dishes of this ware, but many are still more clumsily treated, with a mere outline and a good deal of sponge work; they are occasionally found in cottages along with similar dishes painted with the portraits of William and Mary, Queen Anne, the Duke of Marlborough, and other celebrated personages. This is about the only scriptural subject which was ever a favourite with the English potter, and it is restricted to the decoration of Delft ware. It was probably at first an imitation of some foreign dish that found its way into one of the leading manufactories, and thence was copied over and over again.

The specimen given on this plate was formerly in Professor A. Church's collection.

PL. XXIV.

ENGLISH DELFT PUZZLE JUG.

PLATE XXIV.

ENGLISH DELFT PUZZLE JUG.

HEIGHT 8 INCHES.

T Liverpool the manufacture of Delft ware was so successfully carried on, that for body and glaze it could fairly compare with any of the continental faïence. This puzzle jug is a good though not uncommon example of the Liverpool productions; several others in our collection, exactly similar to this in every other respect, are painted with English verses, and so more obviously show their origin; but here we must remark a particular stiffness in the style of decoration, which, notwithstanding the evident imitation of a Dutch pattern, is very characteristic, and may help to the identification of pieces of a less special shape. The glaze is very brilliant and white, the blue pure in colour, and the clay, probably imported from Holland, friable, and slightly fired. A certain awkwardness in the handling of the brush is often to be noticed on the painted English Delft pieces; at the same time we must bear in mind that upon some authenticated specimens of the Liverpool factories, for instance on *Pennington's* large punch bowls, the painters showed themselves on a level with their foreign rivals.

The making of Delft ware never interfered in England with the development of local productions, which continued to be made with native materials. Seldom do we find English Delft in pieces of general use in the country; for example, few, if any, tea-pots, mugs, or common jugs are to be met with. It was limited rather to fancy articles, such as decorative tiles, vases, and dessert plates; most of it was no doubt exported to the colonies, and the small quantity that remained was spread all over the country, and is now, with few exceptions, mistaken for Dutch ware.

PL. XXV.

ELERS WARE.

PLATE XXV.

ELERS WARE.

HEIGHT 4 INCHES.

INDUSTRIAL art is constantly influenced by circumstances which create fresh wants. French faïence owes its improvements to the ruinous war with Holland; the nobility had to sell their family plate to eke out the failing resources of the king. The potters of Rouen and other places supplied a new kind of earthenware, which, although moderate in price, was not unworthy of having a place upon the table or dresser. When tea was introduced into England, its use at once became so general that cups and teapots could not be imported from China in sufficient quantities; and this new want spreading among all classes of society, a powerful impulse was given to the production of a more delicate and refined sort of ware than that which had been manufactured before for common purposes. The *Elers* having settled in the country at that time, found scope for their art in the imitation of the dainty little vessels then thought indispensable for brewing the costly beverage, and their red tea-pots and cups found a ready market, at very high prices. We here give two specimens of the red porcelain they made in Staffordshire, years before *Bottcher* acquired great celebrity for making the same sort of ware in Germany; it is always unglazed, but the texture is so dense that it can, like the German pieces, be cut and polished on the lapidary's wheel like any hard stone; we have made the experiment ourselves, and it has been attended with success. The etching will show how simple the decoration always was; a branch of tea leaves stamped on the tea-pot, and a conventional flower on the cream jug, were deemed a sufficient ornament; all the merit of these pieces lies in the perfection with which they are thrown and turned, and the finish of the lines of the moulding. Very different from the imitations, these are very thin and sharply made, and we have no hesitation in giving them as genuine examples; a few authenticated bits bearing the same characteristics are preserved in the local museums, mostly toy pieces of diminutive size, sparingly decorated, but no fragments have ever to our knowledge been dug out to enlighten us either upon this red ware or upon any other ware the *Elers* may have manufactured. Tradition has it that they carried away and buried all their imperfect pieces in a distant place. In an expedition to the site of their works which we made in company with Mr. T. Hulme, of Burslem, we found the excavation where they obtained their red clay, but all the diggings we attempted for "vouchers" were completely fruitless, and the oldest people engaged upon the place told us that they did not remember any fragments of pottery having ever been turned out. It is then only by the delicacy of their make that we can, for the present, identify the genuine *Elers* pieces. It has been thought that they were sometimes stamped with a Chinese-looking mark, but the imitations are also marked in the same way.

PL. XXVI.

RED TEAPOT.

PLATE XXVI.

"G. R." RED TEA-POT.

HEIGHT 5 INCHES.

IKE all imitations, this tea-pot comes short of the qualities of the model. The materials are those employed by the *Elers*, and the decoration is stamped with seals in the regular way; it is cleverly turned, and the lid fits to a nicety, but the clay has not been so finely sifted, and the impression lacks the wonted neatness; the side figures show a decided German style; this might lead to the supposition that they were made with old seals borrowed from the foreigners, but in the centre is an allegorical subject, which by the two letters "G R" impressed on the top we may take as representing the marriage of George II.; and there can be no mistake as to the actual date of the piece; besides, the spout and handle are pressed from moulds used for cauliflower tea-pots, and, as we have already remarked, a pressed part is never to be found in the *Elers* ware.

Most of the red pieces that are now mistaken for their work are, like this one, very much later than the early red porcelain of the Dutchmen. A quantity of fragments of engine-turned red ware were dug out from the Bell Works at Burslem, where *Josiah Wedgwood* had his first manufactory, but the body is very inferior in quality.

Pl. XXVII.

Salt-Glaze Teapot.

PLATE XXVII.

SALT-GLAZE TEA-POT,

WITH STAMPED ORNAMENTS.

HEIGHT 6 INCHES.

ASSUMING that the *Elers* made the white or drab Salt-glaze ware in the Staffordshire Potteries, they must have produced pieces similar to this one, so much alike are the ornaments stamped on the turned body and those they used for their red ware. But here again we see that the style of decoration is hardly a safe rule to go by, as imitations were afterwards made presenting the same character. In this example the handle and spout are of the crab-stock pattern, and were cast in a mould; the piece is of a large size and completely white; and all this being considered, we cannot safely attribute it to the Dutchmen. The attribution is less doubtful when we deal with specimens which have the identical ornaments made of white pipe-clay applied upon the drab body; some of them are washed inside with white, and might be for this reason the work of *Astbury*, the immediate successor of the *Elers*. Vine leaves or rosettes are also found on buff pieces as on the early red tea-pots; but the same ornamentation occurs upon cream-colour ware certainly more modern in date, so the puzzle is most perplexing, and only in special cases can it be solved by even an experienced eye.

SALT-GLAZE TEAPOT.

PLATE XXVIII.

SALT-GLAZE SQUARE TEA-POT.

HEIGHT 5½ INCHES.

HE cutting of moulds from a solid mass of gypsum, a method practised for the early pieces of Salt-glaze, must have induced the block cutter to contrive many of his models in a square shape, so much easier was it for him to sink his ornamentation upon flat parts than in the curved surface presented by the hollow fractions of a cylinder. House-shaped tea-pots and other articles were conceived on this principle. In this particular instance four square bats have been sufficient for the construction of the piece; horizontal mouldings cut of a proper size form the foot and the top; the mould has been engraved with a Chinese key running along the principal lines, and the ever-recurring shell. The spout has again the serpent, the arm, and the head of the house-shaped tea-pot, and both may have been the work of the same hand. Before the firing, zaffre was rubbed into the cavities by the process employed for the scratched blue ware; but the piece being of the wafer sort, and the details very sharp, we think it somewhat anterior to the regular scratched blue. Cobalt and zaffre had been but recently introduced in the Potteries, probably in consequence of the trials of Delft ware made by *T. Heath*, of Lane Delph, in 1710. Early pieces of Staffordshire ware do not exhibit a trace of its use, and it is not comprised amongst the metallic oxides that were employed to decorate the Tortoiseshell. It was sparingly applied on the Salt-glaze in the shape of dust long before Cream-colour was painted in blue. Several tea-pots of the same type are in existence; Mr. A. Frank has one upon which the raised pattern has the delicacy of the work of a silversmith.

SALT-GLAZE GROUP.

PLATE XXIX.

SALT-GLAZE GROUP.

HEIGHT 5 INCHES.

T is surprising to find such a piece as this, evidently the fruit of a whimsical imagination, to which no special purpose can be attributed, made at a time when modelling was confined to the raised ornaments which were sparingly used to complete smoothly-turned shapes, and when fancy could only exercise itself on the commonest articles of daily use. We may ask ourselves whether this dignified lady and gentleman, attired in their Sunday clothes, and resting upon their homely settle, are the portraits of "the Squire and his wife," or merely the fanciful creation of the maker's inventive mind? If the latter, the choice of the subject may be said to be quite on a level with its primitive execution, and the style of modelling had to undergo a great and rapid change before the modellers of the Potteries could produce the varied, ingenious, and clever figures which were made a few years afterwards.

We can see by the awkwardness of this group that it was not a common practice at that time to turn out a work of this kind; the costumes of the figures refer it to the period of Slip dishes, and it suggests to us the idea of *Thomas Toft* trying his hand at sculpture. The piece is entirely made by hand, with the white stone body of Staffordshire, but it has the peculiarity of being partially coloured with patches of brown, made with the oxide of iron used for the brown ware of Nottingham, a combination seldom if ever before met with. This fact throws a doubt upon its origin, but we have no hesitation in saying that it is one of the earliest examples of Salt-glaze.

PL. XXX.

SALT-GLAZE TEAPOT.

PLATE XXX.

SALT-GLAZE HOUSE TEA-POT.

HEIGHT 5 INCHES.

LARGE numbers of Salt-glaze tea-pots were made in the shape of a house, sometimes having the royal arms over the door, and a sentry on each side, but more frequently reproducing some private dwelling.

Considering how proud a man is when he builds a house of his own, and how every allusion to the subject pleasantly tickles his vanity, may not such a piece have been thought an appropriate present to offer to a friend on such an occasion? What gives weight to our supposition with regard to these numerous tea-pots is, that they are never made to represent a curious building, or an ambitious palace, but the square and common-place home of a well-to-do Englishman.

Without asserting that every Staffordshire tea-pot was intended to convey a special meaning, we must admit, from many examples, that people in olden times were often prompted to embody their thoughts in a tangible shape—what they could not write they expressed in a graphic form. Lovers offered to each other a symbolical tea-pot in the shape of a heart; for the man of politics there was the tea-pot commemorating a successful election, or a great victory like the taking of Portobello by Admiral Vernon; and we are not at all sure that the Bacchus tea-pot was not a sarcastic present to an habitual drunkard, forestalling in this forcible way the teachings of "teetotalism."

The spout of the specimen here produced presents a mysterious riddle; it is formed by a stretched hand holding a serpent; on the lower part grins a curious head. The meaning of this, if indeed it has any, we cannot fathom, and will not try to explain.

Pl. XXXI.

SALT-GLAZE TEAPOT.

PLATE XXXI.

FOUR-LOBED TEA-POT.

HEIGHT $4\frac{1}{2}$ INCHES.

NE could not imagine a more dainty little piece; it was well adapted to its probable use, and made a charming present to a lady. The fact of its coming from an outlandish district rather enhanced its value and interest in the eyes of the fair Londoner. A replica of the same model in our collection is enamelled with a subject in colour, and is a complete representation of English ceramic art at its best. We also possess a smaller four-lobed tea-pot, but of a straight shape, resting on three delicate claws, and embossed with the usual group of shells, oak leaves, and acorns; parts are stained with blue, and the details are very sharply cut. Is it a toy, a gimcrack, or a tea-pot? It is rather difficult to decide.

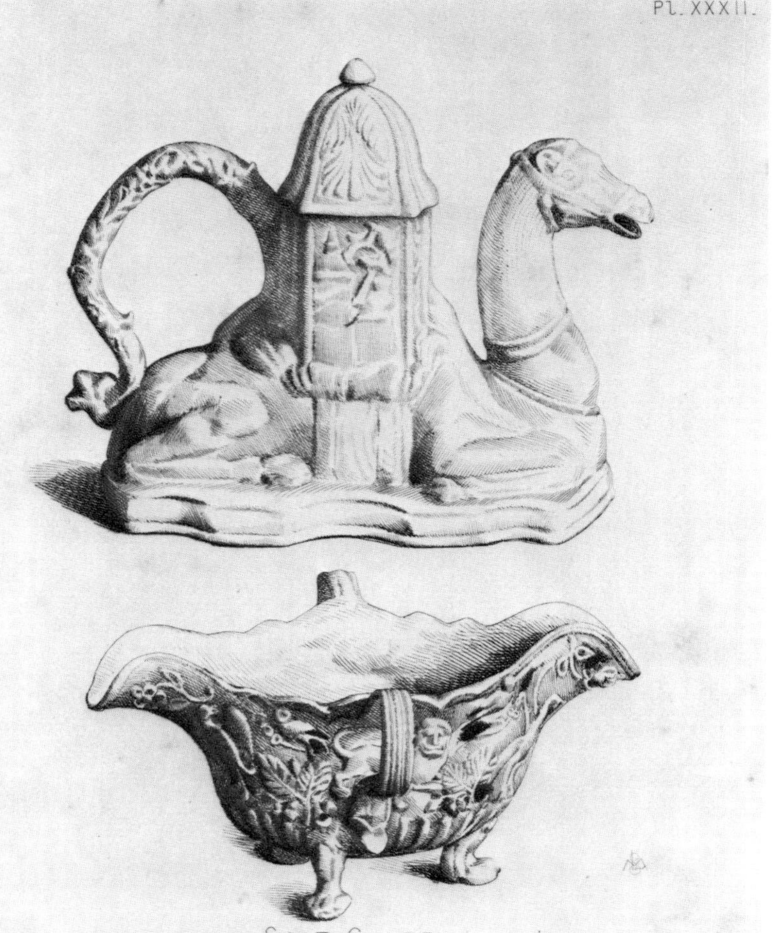

PL. XXXII.

SALT-GLAZE.
CAMEL TEA-POT AND SAUCE BOAT.

PLATE XXXII.

CAMEL TEA-POT. SAUCE BOAT.

HEIGHT 5 INCHES. HEIGHT 3 INCHES.

EW shapes were required to set forth in all its originality the new Salt-glaze ware, which was from the first manufactured with materials so different from those which had been used before; public taste had already got tired of globular shapes turned on the wheel, and having a uniform profile, either left plain or insufficiently diversified by applications of meagre flowers or leaves. The secret of the manufacture of white ware could not long be kept amongst a few, but soon became public property, and the competing potters had to exercise their wits in bringing out striking novelties, endeavouring in that way to outdo each other. The imagination of modellers on their mettle gave vent to all sorts of inventions, verging sometimes on extravagance; and the process of casting lately introduced permitted them to execute their most complicated conceptions. There was no natural object, no impracticable representation of animal or figure that was not thought fit to be turned into a tea-pot. A camel, for instance, could not at first sight be considered a very promising subject for that purpose. Perhaps on this account it was often preferred, and the difficulties surmounted in different ways. The one shown on this plate represents a camel of a rather naturalistic shape, but others combine, in a highly conventional style, the ribs of the shell pattern with the general outlines of the kneeling animal. Squirrels, bears, cats, and other animals were also adapted, and were in all cases made ornamental with scrolls or flowers embossed all over, thus avoiding the ludicrous effect always evinced by a too realistic production.

Underneath is a small sauce-boat resting on three claws; this is of an earlier period. It is one of those pieces which, by their shape and their overcrowded decoration, have led to the supposition that sometimes discarded moulds from some silversmith's manufactory were used for the making of Salt-glaze ware; but a cursory examination will suffice to show that the subjects were carved in the style of the block-cutter, and do not resemble the chasing of plate; they present only the outward likeness that the works of the same epoch and country bear to each other. This specimen is decorated with a lion, an eagle, and the nondescript bird which is often taken to be the liver of the Liverpool arms, combined with foliage and flowers. It is as delicate in its make as a silver piece, and small patches of blue paste have been interspersed at random amongst the raised ornamentation. Later on blue paste was used to apply neat blue relief upon the white ground.

Sauce-boats, tea ware, and pickle trays were the first productions of the improving Potteries, and very especial care was bestowed upon them, to wit, the remarkable piece belonging to Professor A. Church, upon which the Seven Champions of Christendom are elaborately represented. Table ware was only attempted much later on; even at the Worcester China Manufactory they avoided in the first years making anything of large size; and some contemporaries expressed their astonishment at the want of enterprise of the English China makers, who had not so far tried to compete with the plates and dishes imported from the East, the only ones that could then be procured for dinner services.

Pl. XXXIII.

SALT-GLAZE TEAPOT.

PLATE XXXIII.

SALT-GLAZE SHELL TEA-POT.

HEIGHT 5 INCHES.

HIS piece is one of the most strikingly typical examples of the mould-cutter's art, and plainly illustrates the peculiar style of an ornamentation sunk and engraved, and how it differs from modelled relief. The oval shape was first chosen, as being more convenient to be worked out in two pieces, instead of three, which the making of a circular form would necessitate. No foot or separate neck has been added to the simple, purse-like profile, these would have created a difficulty in the casting; but to take away its plainness and make it pleasing and handsome, the form was carved in the hollow with all the devices that could be easily produced with the burin. The pecten shell was peculiarly adapted for this sort of work; we can see how each rib was readily formed by one single stroke of the tool, and how in the same way the flowers and snakes that appear on the piece could easily be made. The mould-cutter frequently availed himself of the fitness of the ribbed shell for his requirements, and there are indeed very few specimens of early Salt-glaze ware upon which it does not play the most important part in the decoration.

PL. XXXIV.

SALT GLAZE COFFEE POT.

PLATE XXXIV.

SALT-GLAZE COFFEE-POT.

HEIGHT 7½ INCHES.

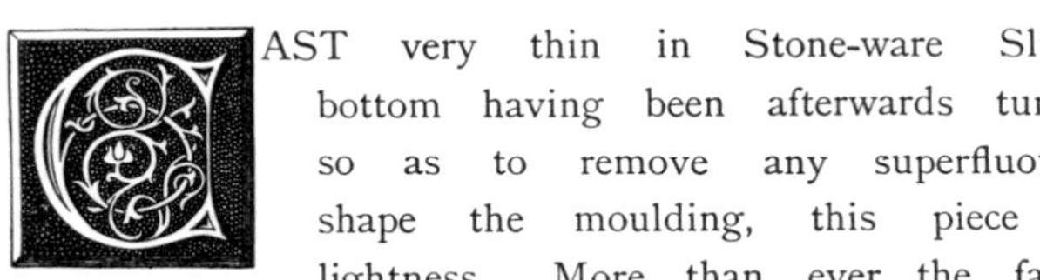

CAST very thin in Stone-ware Slip, the top and bottom having been afterwards turned on the lathe, so as to remove any superfluous substance and shape the moulding, this piece is of surprising lightness. More than ever the familiar pecten shell has been brought into requisition; a number of them of various forms and dimensions were disposed somewhat in the same way as the conventional honeysuckle is arranged in Greek ornament. The mould had to be combined in three parts, and each was treated as an independent panel, separated from the next by the seam, which remained apparent, and thus some advantage was derived from one of the necessities of fabrication. In our time, the line marked by the junction of the mould would have been considered as very objectionable, and all possible means would have been taken to conceal it under an ineffectual combination of details. The pot rests on three claws, resembling those seen on the silver pieces of that time, and the handle is made by hand with a flat strip of clay, bent to suit the shape, and pinched with the fingers at the lower part. Although the earliest models with compartments may all be similar in design, we have always noticed that each compartment was carved separately, with slight variations of lines; never were they obtained by an impression of the first one; this last device, on the contrary, was always practised as soon as plaster moulds were brought into use.

Pl. XXXV.

Salt-Glaze Teapot.

PLATE XXXV.

OCTAGONAL SALT-GLAZE TEA-POT.

HEIGHT 4½ INCHES.

HEN a piece was intended to be produced by casting, the model was seldom made of a round shape; for these latter, turning, with application of stamped ornament, was generally preferred; for a cast piece, pentagonal and lobed shapes were combined, and the seams of the mould were, as we have already remarked, used to divide the sections from each other by raised lines. In this instance eight panels were necessary to complete the tea-pot, and the seams have been contrived so as to form vertical mouldings carefully connected with the corresponding horizontal lines.

We cannot discover any connection between the complicated subjects carved round this specimen; and the etching need not be supplemented by any description beyond saying that, from the style of panelling, the mixture of mythological figures, fables, *Renaissance* animals, and the arms of France, seen on both sides, we fancy they must have been borrowed from some carved oak chest of French origin. Delicate cups and saucers, and octagonal jugs, belonging to the same set, but having a great variety of figures and ornaments, are sometimes found; of this sort is also the celebrated Shakespeare jug.

Amongst the blocks lately added to our collection is one of those from which these same tea-pots were made. It came from Enoch Wood's Museum, and was kindly presented to us by Messrs. Minton; it is of hard yellow Stone-ware, and is not glazed with salt, as we generally find them. Upon such blocks moulds were pressed in clay, and after having been fired they were practically indestructible; sometimes the clay was only dried. An old workman of Hanley was, a few years ago, still casting very neat pieces in moulds of dry clay, by what he called the old process.

Many of the old routine ways have long continued in the Potteries, and have outlived the new-fangled fashions which successively give way to one another; consequently from the mere make of a particular specimen, to fix the period to which it belongs is often a matter of guess-work, and in the absence of a date never goes beyond mere probability. We possess an earthenware cream jug, also in eight compartments, with embossed subjects. The mould was constructed on the old system, and the piece, thinly cast and not pressed, has all the characteristics of an early specimen; the little figures, very numerous and varied, are as sharp in detail and quaint in design as on the finest models of Salt-glaze, and the whole is touched up with tortoiseshell colours. Two initials, "H. R.," are scratched under the bottom, and the top has the name of "*John Lucas*" painted in blue. This shows the jug to be a presentation piece, and we may take it to be the work of an old workman, who was pleased to revive for once the best fashions of his younger days; otherwise, were we to consider it a regular production of the period, when finding it, to our amazement, dated as late as 1790, nothing would remain for the collector but to declare his utter incapability to distinguish such ware from what was manufactured in the beginning of the same century.

PL. XXXVI.

SALT-GLAZE MUG.

TEA CADDY.

PLATE XXXVI.

"G. R." SALT-GLAZE MUG.

HEIGHT 6 INCHES.

HEAD TEA-CADDY.

HOUGH evidently made with the view of competing with the Stone-ware imported from Germany, this mug is thinner and whiter than the pieces it strove to emulate; it is likewise incised with deep lines, coloured over with dark blue, and has a raised medallion of the king stuck on the central part. The imitation is by no means a servile one; the body is the same as that used for the ordinary Salt-glaze pieces, and does not resemble the Flemish grey stone-ware, of which many examples, also stamped with the monogram "G. R.," remain for comparison; the decoration is clumsy, being even below the awkward scrawling seen on the English scratched blue, the colour having been only coarsely spread with a rag soaked in cobalt. Usually these pieces are attributed to Fulham, but we know that a much better imitation of the foreign article was produced there, and fragments dug up in the Staffordshire Potteries warrant our supposing that they were manufactured in that locality.

Jugs, mugs, and jars are frequently met with, and they are all cleverly thrown, turned, and handled. They were, no doubt, commonly made for the use of public-houses, and bear the royal effigy, with the monogram "G. R.," which stood then as a guarantee of their being of the legal capacity. We think they must be referred to the reign of George II. or George III. A small jug in the Liverpool Museum, identical in body and shape with the piece represented in this plate, is said to have been made by *J. Malkin*, in 1690; but little reliance can be placed on a family tradition which no other facts come to corroborate.

We give on the same plate a curious tea-caddy of cream-colour earthenware, of which more will be said when we describe the head tea-pot belonging to the same set.

SALT-GLAZE BASKET.

PLATE XXXVII.

SALT-GLAZE BASKET.

LENGTH 13 INCHES.

Y slow degrees the middle class became used to more refinement in the service of the table. From Germany the finest samples of Continental porcelain were daily brought over, amongst them dessert plates and dishes elegantly perforated. For the modest admirer who could not afford the expense of such costly luxuries, fruit baskets and plates, cut out with an equal delicacy, were manufactured in Salt-glaze ware, and being comparatively cheap, met with a ready sale. Some were made like real baskets, others with open fancy work, the intricacy of the design dispensing with any addition of painting or gilding. The one we give on this plate shows the peculiarity that, while the ornamentation of the outside is obtained by the casting of the piece in a plaster mould, the inside is stamped over with groups of flowers impressed by means of brass seals, thus uniting the early process with the new one, and showing the superiority of the earlier for neatness of execution. Most delicate perforations were also practised upon thinly-turned pieces with iron tools, cutting out the hole at once in the required shape; so by "punching," as it was called, the top of a jug or the rim of a plate could, with very little trouble, be made to look marvellously worked. Some of the smallest pieces of basket work were pressed in brass moulds, but the use of these was restricted to the making of minute articles, which could be stamped at one blow, such as spoons, pickle leaves, or diminutive gadrooned cups; in this case the embossments show on both sides of the piece, one being the counterpart of the other. Baskets were also made in tortoiseshell, but more especially in cream-coloured ware, and at a later period became a very important item amongst the productions of the English potter.

Salt-Glaze Soup Tureen.

Pl. XXXVIII.

PLATE XXXVIII.

SALT-GLAZE SOUP TUREEN.

LENGTH 11 INCHES.

REPLICA of the soup tureen here represented is now in the Jermyn Street Museum; it bears the date, 1763, and the initials "J. B." scratched in the clay at the bottom. These two letters might stand for the name of *John Baddeley*, who was at that time one of the best potters of Staffordshire, and was making ware of precisely the same description; we cannot say positively that it may be considered as his mark, but in support of such a supposition, we can identify the pattern as being the work of *Aaron Wood*, the modeller he employed, and who has signed with his name more than one block belonging to the same set. It is the same basket-work (diaper of dots and conventional leaves) which was so often repeated upon all sorts of table ware. It is a late piece, and although the ornaments have been sunk in the mould after the old style, it is thick and coarsely cast; the moulding is no longer finished on the lathe, and the ornaments have lost their sharpness. It is by no means an uncommon specimen; we have ourselves seen many similar ones, but in all these the knobs and claws were very different; this might be explained by the fact that pieces of this kind were produced by more than one maker.

That soup tureens were so extensively made is not easily reconcilable with the notion that soup appeared on the table of very few Englishmen of the time, and would show that Salt-glaze was intended for the upper classes. The names under which they are designated in the old accounts is the French word "*terrine*," an earthen basin, which subsequently was altered into tureen. Pickle trays are also described from the French as "*hors-d'œuvre*."

SALT-GLAZE MUG.

PLATE XXXIX.

MIDNIGHT CONVERSATION—SALT-GLAZE MUG.

HEIGHT 7 INCHES.

OW deceptive a style of ornamentation may prove if by it alone we try to determine the age of a piece of earthenware! Looking at the profusion of uncouth birds, reptiles, and quadrupeds spread all over the sides of this mug, and the stiff border of nondescript flowers arranged on its base, we could not help surmising that it was a work inspired by the illumination of some mediæval MS., and contemporaneous with the old missals; yet, in the centre has been reproduced a comparatively modern picture by Hogarth; its title, "Midnight Conversation," has been engraved underneath, to prevent any doubt in that respect. The modeller was at no pains to modify his Gothic manner when engaged in imitating the principal features of the well-known composition; it is a free and easy adaptation, and all the personages, notwithstanding their periwigs and tobacco pipes, have a decidedly Byzantine appearance. Could such primitive-looking images have been perpetrated in London after 1750, the date of the publication of Hogarth's engraving, where artists lived surrounded by the best works of the time?

A mug precisely similar to this, now in Lady Charlotte Schreiber's possession, was found amongst the pieces discovered in the cellars of the old Fulham works, and consequently has been attributed to that manufacture. Many reasons would induce us to suppose that it was not made there, but in the Potteries. The ware is exactly like the

Salt-glaze ware of Staffordshire. In the Stoke Museum may be seen a large cream-colour punch bowl, decorated over the glaze with the same "Midnight Conversation," still an adaptation of the original, but painted in black and red in a less barbarous manner. Taking for granted that it is the work of a local artist, we can infer from it that the subject was then a favourite one. But the most striking evidence in support of our supposition is the presence on the piece of four coats of arms, three of them belonging to Staffordshire families—*Hales, Baronet*, *Leveson-Gower*, *Vane*, and *Bertie*. Another Salt-glaze mug of the same size and shape, but with a totally different decoration, had the portrait of George II., inscribed "*God save the King and my Master,*" surrounded with the same escutcheons as above, with two more in addition, also connected with Staffordshire—*Whorewood* and *Granville*.

This was not the only piece found at Fulham which had no connection with the productions of *John Dwight*. Like the Salt-glaze sauce-boat and others, it had been bought as a model, probably at the time when *Mr. White*, having married Margaret Dwight, re-established the factory after the former owners had become bankrupts in 1747. Copies of the subject are found upon pieces of the regular Fulham stone-ware, dating from the end of the 18th century.

We know of more than one copy of the same mug. Such a handsome piece of ware must always have been considered a great curiosity, and had a better chance of being carefully preserved than an ordinary mug or tea-pot. The Liverpool Museum has one of great beauty, and the one here reproduced comes from the Hamilton Palace collection.

SCRATCHED BLUE POSSET-POT.

PLATE XL.

SCRATCHED BLUE POSSET POT.

HEIGHT 9½ INCHES.

HE skilful turning of this piece is inconsistent with a very early date of manufacture, but, as a contrast, the decoration is so barbarous that many would not hesitate to refer it to the remotest infancy of art. When an article had to be finished off with "scratched blue," it was, as soon as the turner had done with it, handed to the "flowerer," a woman or an apprentice, who, with an iron point, scratched in the clay a few scrolls and flowers of her own imagining, without any guidance from a pattern. Powdered zaffre or smalt, that is to say a sort of glass coloured with cobalt, that for cheapness sake the potters used for a long time in preference to the expensive oxide, was dabbed into the incised lines with a flock of cotton wool. Fancy pieees were principally decorated, such as posset pots, or loving cups, puzzle jugs, spirit flasks, or presentation mugs. We assisted in the unearthing, in some excavations at Hanley, of an enormous heap of diminutive cups without handles, and saucers as thin as egg-shell china, all broken to fragments, and which had been thrown away as imperfect; from this we may see that the makers of scratched blue had great difficulties to contend with.

The white Salt-glaze pieces which came out of the mould covered with embossments, and were produced by the hundred, left the casting shop completely finished, and no particular handiwork distinguished one from the other. The scratched blue, on the contrary, had to receive a fancy decoration, which could in each instance be made different, and often, as a matter of course, the workman supplemented his design with inscriptions of names and dates. Thus it happens that, while the white pieces are seldom, if ever, inscribed, the blue ones are generally so, and many examples are dated from 1750 to 1780.

Wedgwood, it is said, began by making this sort of ware during his first partnership with *Harrison*, of Stoke. We can imagine what must have been his dismay when, after he had caused a piece to be thrown and turned with the greatest care and precision, he saw it thus scrawled over by inexperienced hands. Was it from this that during his whole career he decidedly preferred the repeated reproduction of a work modelled under his own eyes by select sculptors to any painting that could be freely executed upon a plain surface?

ENAMELLED SALT-GLAZE JUG.

PLATE XLI.

ENAMELLED SALT-GLAZE JUG.

HEIGHT 8½ INCHES.

DMIRABLY potted and turned, as delicately pencilled as any costly piece of English china, the brilliancy of the enamels contrasting charmingly with the subdued white tint of its ground, this jug is one of the best representatives of enamelled Salt-glaze ware. The decoration of a pseudo-Chinese character recalls the art of the Dutch painters, who, after having studied the porcelain of China, rather than copy any special design, let their fancy run loose upon subjects of their own imagination. We have seen, and possess ourselves, many nice specimens of the same ware, but none that come up to this standard. It was probably the work of two clever Dutchmen who settled at Hot Lane, near Burslem, and there, buying white pieces from the local potters, inaugurated a new style of painting, soon imitated all over the district, and which was applied not only to Salt-glaze but also to cream-coloured earthenware.

Pl. XLII.

Tortoiseshell Posset Pot.

PLATE XLII.

TORTOISESHELL POSSET POT.

HEIGHT 7½ INCHES.

Y this time foreign wines and handsome light cups had replaced, in the improved household, the homely ale and the heavy posset pot. The fastidiousness of the educated man, which would have been shocked by the coarse tyg of dark clay, could be adequately gratified by so nicely-made a piece of bright earthenware; by its elegance of shape and delicacy of relief work, it served creditably in lieu of the china or silver bowl, luxuries possessed by only a very few.

All round the cup a climbing vine spreads its branches and tendrils; to the stems, made by hand, leaves and bunches of grapes have been stuck at intervals; if any meaning is attached to this decoration, we may suppose that the time-honoured beer and spice mixture was not to be brewed in this vessel. Manganese and copper green, applied in unequal patches, have softly run down with the flowing glaze, and form a subdued harmony with the cream-colour of the ground. As we have already remarked, tortoiseshell ware was not peculiar to one maker, but was produced with more or less ability in every pot works in Staffordshire.

Contrary to the practice on the Continent, where each manufacturer limited himself to a speciality, the English potter had always a great variety of bodies and glazes to work with at one and the same time. Along the Rhine is found the Grès Stone-ware, and in Holland the white faïence with a stanniferous glaze; each factory of Italy kept to a special style of decoration, almost sufficient for identification, and a great difference distinguishes one French ware from another. If we take such potters as *Astbury*, *Whieldon*, and their contemporaries, we find that within their small premises all sorts of ware were concurrently manufactured—red or black body, either dry or glazed; white stone-ware glazed with salt or with lead; cream-colour, plain, and coloured with tortoiseshell enamels; even, in a few instances, Delft-ware with blue painting; and when we come to the study of *Josiah Wedgwood's* works, we are amazed at the endless variety of bodies he was continually busy in creating and improving.

PL. XLIII.

AGATE-WARE TEAPOT.

PLATE XLIII.

AGATE-WARE TEA-POT.

HEIGHT 6 INCHES.

HIS tea-pot, of which replicas are often met with, is one of the nicest pieces of Agate-ware that ever came under our notice. We have already described how the body was prepared by laying upon each other thin alternate layers of white and red clay; a sufficient mass being thus obtained, it was vertically cut through with a wire into thin bats, and these were formed into shape by careful pressing in a mould. When dry, they were finished and polished on the lathe, and either glazed in their natural colours, red and yellow, or different shades of brown and red, or else stained with a blue glaze, which imparted to the mixture the fine greyish hue of agate. Pieces of a small size alone, such as tea ware, pickle trays, sauce boats, and snuff boxes, were made of these mixed bodies. Seldom do they show any embossment; round pieces got a better surface by turning, and our example is an exception to the general rule. Its shape is ribbed in imitation of the shell tea-pots then commonly made in Salt-glaze, but without any of their intricate details; a flat slice of marbled clay could not have been forced into narrow cavities without losing its fine veining through the requisite manipulation, consequently the original shape has been rounded, softened, and smoothed, to facilitate the pressing. It is worth noticing that these Agate-ware pieces are certainly anterior in date to the supposed introduction of the process of pressing in the Staffordshire Potteries. We may hazard the supposition that casting and throwing were preferred as a rule, and that pressing was confined to a limited use long before it became generally employed at the time fixed by tradition.

The knife hafts so extensively manufactured by *Dr. Thomas Wedgwood* and *Whieldon* for the cutlers of Sheffield are precisely similar in body and glaze to this specimen, and we may refer it to one of these two potters, probably the latter, considering its perfection. The innovation introduced in the making of Agate-ware, by which it differs from the mixed clays employed a very long time before, is the transverse cutting through of the mass with a wire, which gave a fineness and continuity to the lines of the marbling unobtainable by the ordinary mode of blending the clays, and the pressing in a mould instead of throwing on the wheel, by which the veining was disturbed. At Fulham, *Dwight* produced a sort of Agate-ware, with grey and white Stone-ware; and many common pieces of the same period are streaked with light and dark clays. Early in Staffordshire different coloured clays were also blended together in a rough way, so as to imitate marble; in that manner large slabs were made, some destined to be inserted in the walls of houses, relating the name of the owner and the year of construction; others with inscriptions scratched in, or laid on with slip, were set up over graves; some of these are still to be seen in the churchyards of the Potteries.

In Italy and in France, as well as in Germany, mixed bodies were frequently employed; it is interesting, for instance, to compare the English Agate-ware with what was done, nearly in the same style, in the factories of Apt, in Provence, towards the end of the 18th century.

PL. XLIV.

PERFORATED TORTOISESHELL TEA-POT.

PLATE XLIV.

PERFORATED TORTOISESHELL TEA-POT.

HEIGHT 6 INCHES.

HIELDON, like his predecessors, looked upon Chinese ware as the best model a potter could emulate; but instead of being content with a mere imitation of the commonest productions of the East in the simple way that had so far been followed, he endeavoured to reproduce those which looked most complicated. This tea-pot, which can be attributed to him, is evidently copied from or suggested by an Oriental piece. It is made in a double shell, the outer one being perforated according to a design of leaves and apple blossoms disposed for that purpose; this cutting out covers the shape with a sort of lace-work, very light in appearance, and the peculiar tints of English tortoiseshell-ware impart to the whole a look of originality which makes one forget that the piece was an imitation. Perforated tea-pots of the same description are also found in a dry red body. The effect produced by that outward piercing is at once so charming and surprising to one who does not comprehend how it can be executed, that we have seen the process revived many times at different places, and always given out as a fresh invention.

BLACK WARE AND TORTOISESHELL.

PLATE XLV.

BLACK TEA-POT.

TORTOISESHELL TEA-POT.

HEIGHT 3½ INCHES.

COMPROMISE was soon established between the common pieces of dark clay glazed with galena, and the more refined ware of dry red colour, finely turned and neatly stamped, which, in the hands of the *Elers*, had for a time defied comparison with any other manufacture. Small pieces began to be made with the materials previously used for large tygs; they were turned on the lathe, and adorned with applications of variously-coloured clays. *Astbury* was probably the first who glazed the red body of the Dutchmen, and relieved it with ornaments of white clay. It is interesting to follow the efforts of the early potter, who, unable to diversify his productions by painting or hand decoration, had to contrive all sorts of combinations of clays to give them a little variety. On this little tea-pot white leaves have been stamped on the background; very different in effect are those which in our collection belong to the same period; they present all possible arrangements of buff, dark yellow, red, brown, and white, being sometimes finished off with a few touches of underglaze colours. The reliefs are often stamped in white on a black ground; in this case they were decorated with size gilding, or gold-leaf fixed with a hard varnish. It was only towards the end of the 18th century that the burning in of the gold was known in the Potteries. Imperfect as this mode of gilding may have been, yet it had one quality, it was transparent and mellow in colour, and looked certainly more like the Oriental gold than the burnished metal employed later on upon china; on most pieces it has now disappeared, and this one has only kept a few traces of it.

The regular imitation of tortoiseshell was practised upon cream-colour pieces, generally sprigged on with reliefs of rosettes, or branches and flowers. Manganese and a small sponge to apply it in irregular spots were the only requisites. The fire causing the spots of oxide to run into each other sufficed to give to this simple process an appearance of finish, and to imitate the delicate gradation of tints noticeable on the genuine material.

PL. XLVI.

WHIELDON JUG.

PLATE XLVI.

WHIELDON JUG.

HEIGHT $7\frac{1}{2}$ INCHES.

BY a piece of rare good fortune we have been able to identify this Jug as *Whieldon's* own manufacture. The pedigree is a very humble one, but the piece has its credentials. It was made in 1757 for one Ralph Hammersley, who was, we are sorry to say, not a man of great mark, but merely *Whieldon's* milkman! Anything better made than this jug cannot be imagined; it is as thin and true as if it were made of metal, and the raised decoration, all applied by hand, is artistically arranged. The flowers are tinted with grey, yellow, and green glazes; the monogram and date are painted with red clay, a combination of processes not uncommonly seen on the works of this potter.

Tortoiseshell pieces are very varied in effects; either the whole surface is hidden under dark and powerful colours, manganese and dark grey predominating, or, as in the present instance, the light yellow clay is left to appear everywhere, and only the reliefs are touched up with cloudy and transparent tints; these latter are generally of the best make and of a late period.

The method of applying or "sprigging" the reliefs pressed in separate moulds of highly-fired clay is one of the great characteristics of English pottery. It continued to be practised after the plaster moulds had come into use, and *Wedgwood* adhered to it for his Jasper ware; in no other way could he have obtained the unrivalled sharpness of his raised figures and ornamentation.

PL. XLVII.

TORTOISESHELL FIGURES.

PLATE XLVII.

TORTOISESHELL FIGURE.

HEIGHT 13½ INCHES.

TOBY JUG.

HEIGHT 9½ INCHES.

URING the early Salt-glaze and tortoiseshell period figures were rarely attempted; their modelling is but one degree higher than *Thomas Toft's* painting in slip; nevertheless a bit of old pitcher may please us by its unpretentious oddity, and we cannot think of lamenting the absence of classical learning; it makes up in "näivete" for what it lacks in correctness. Such pieces could not have become articles of regular trade, clumsily made up, as they were, of separate parts, some of them pressed in moulds, while the others were made by hand. The huntsman sketched on this plate was in that manner constructed piecemeal; the hat, gun, and plinth were modelled with various clays, while the rest, which is in the common earthenware body, was pressed, each limb separately, the whole being finally stuck together and coloured over with manganese. *Whieldon* had a speciality for little figures of variegated colours; a very characteristic one was a little horseman, the figure made of cream-colour, richly painted with green, yellow, and brown, and the horse of black clay, with white trappings. It was only when plaster moulds allowed of more complicated subjects being produced that greater care was bestowed upon the modelling of figures; some, like the one belonging to Mr. Soden Smith, were copied after Watteau or other celebrated artists.

But although continuing to be decorated by the old tortoiseshell method, they must certainly be considered as more modern than those made in pieces with light and dark clays.

The next piece is one of the numerous varieties of Toby Jugs or Toby Fill-pots, as they are sometimes called. It is a descendant of the old "greybeard;" little by little the mask that grins on the neck of the ancient beer-bottel was transformed into the more genial face of a toper, and the body of the jug itself cut out in the shape of a stout old man. This one is made of several coloured clays, and for this reason may be of early date; but many, and these are of recent date, are found painted under or over the glaze. These jugs have been constantly manufactured up to our own day.

Pl. XLVIII.

CAULIFLOWER WARE.

PLATE XLVIII.

CAULIFLOWER WARE.

HEIGHT 10 INCHES.

FRENCH author says that he who creates a new proverb does more for humanity than they who write exhaustive books; in the same way, a man who invents a new type might be said to do more towards improving the art of his time than another who achieves a skilful and elaborate work. This, we think, holds good with respect to the industrial artist who chances to hit upon an idea so well calculated to please that its success will afford employment to a large number of his fellows. How many workmen in the Potteries were kept employed in reproducing the first cauliflower pieces, the happy thought of some unknown block cutter! Considering the means at the potter's disposal, it would hardly have been possible to show them to better advantage; cream-colour and green glaze are specially adapted to transforming into a ceramic work of art this common vegetable. The idea was turned to all sorts of purposes, and for a time all the makers manufactured cauliflower ware with ever-increasing success. From this was derived a series of different fruit wares—pine-apple, melons, etc., which in turn stimulated the public taste for novelty, and by their large sale had no doubt an important share in the extension of trade that took place at that time. They are all pressed in terra-cotta moulds, which preserve to the end the fineness of the details, and the brightness of their colour would strengthen the supposition that it was with the view of improving such pieces that *Wedgwood* compounded his celebrated green glaze when he was in partnership with *Whieldon*.

Pl. XLIX.

BRACKETS.

PLATE XLIX.

BRACKETS.

HEIGHT 8½ INCHES.

LITTLE can be said about these brackets; the maker is unknown, and their fabric is similar to that of the pieces already described. They are of the dark tortoise-shell sort; the ornamental part of the first being thickly covered with deep brown and green glazes; the head is left the colour of the clay, and the eyeballs are painted with red slip, in the usual fashion. The ground of the other is of a lighter grey, and the bird of a bright yellow. Hanging spill vases, like mantel-piece ornaments, mark the period when a more refined class of ware came to be in demand. The same models are often found in Salt-glaze ware, and of several sizes.

CREAM-COLOUR TEAPOT.

PLATE L.

HEAD TEA-POT.

HEIGHT 6 INCHES.

EVIDENTLY cut by a working potter, and not modelled by an educated artist, this quaint tea-pot is remarkable for a feeling of originality, not at all lessened because the maker may have been actuated by the idea of emulating some antique vessel once seen and almost forgotten. The head, perhaps a local portrait, has the English periwig; the peculiar notching of the eyebrows and the character of the ornamentation exclude the supposition of it being a copy, but, as is the case with the Greek sculptures, an unconscious simplification in the rendering of natural forms changes into a work of high art that which, in a more realistic period, would only be vulgarity and grotesque fancy; it is in this respect nearer to the works of the ancients than many other pieces which can boast of being more faithful reproductions. It is one of a set of three pieces, made of coarse cream ware, and coloured with tortoiseshell glazes. A tea-caddy, also a portrait, has been reproduced on another plate.

Not long after this, many mugs and two-handled cups were made in the shape of heads, a Satyr, a Bacchus, or sometimes a worthy personage, with the name stamped on the rim; but few exhibit such a conventionality of treatment; and this, in our estimation, renders this set particularly interesting.